MAKE YOUR OWN TWINE GAMES!

MAKE YOUR OWN TWINE GAMES!

ANNA ANTHROPY

no starch press

San Francisco

Printed in USA

First printing

23 22 21 20 19 1 2 3 4 5 6 7 8 9

ISBN-10: 1-59327-938-8
ISBN-13: 978-1-59327-938-7

Publisher: William Pollock
Production Editor: Laurel Chun
Cover Illustration: Josh Ellingson
Illustrator: Caitlin Rose Boyle
Developmental Editor: Annie Choi
Technical Reviewer: Kyle Reimergartin
Copyeditor: Anne Marie Walker
Compositor: Happenstance Type-O-Rama
Proofreader: Emelie Burnette

For information on distribution, translations, or bulk sales, please contact No Starch Press, Inc. directly:
No Starch Press, Inc.
245 8th Street, San Francisco, CA 94103
phone: 1.415.863.9900; info@nostarch.com
www.nostarch.com

Library of Congress Cataloging-in-Publication Data

Names: Anthropy, Anna, author.
Title: Make your own Twine games! / Anna Anthropy.
Description: San Francisco : No Starch Press, 2019.
Identifiers: LCCN 2018055988 (print) | LCCN 2018056958 (ebook) | ISBN 9781593279394 (epub) | ISBN 9781593279387 (paperback) | ISBN 1593279388 (print)
Subjects: LCSH: Video games--Programming--Juvenile literature. | Video games--Authorship--Juvenile literature. | Twine (Computer program)--Juvenile literature. | BISAC: COMPUTERS / Programming / Games. | GAMES / Video & Electronic. | COMPUTERS / Programming / General.
Classification: LCC QA76.76.C672 (ebook) | LCC QA76.76.C672 A5847 2019 (print) | DDC 794.8/1525--dc23
LC record available at https://lccn.loc.gov/2018055988

For the new generation, and
for the generation who grew up
without having the tools:
Here they are.

About the Author

ANNA ANTHROPY is a game designer, author, and educator. She lives in Chicago with her little black cat, Encyclopedia Frown, where she teaches game design as DePaul University's Game Designer in Residence.

About the Technical Reviewer

KYLE REIMERGARTIN is a parent and a second-grade teacher. He makes computer games, pies, zines, and tapes. Some of his favorite subjects to incorporate into his games include skin, places, rituals, doors, germs, teeth, and cats. He is the creator of *Fjords,* and he's currently developing a game called *Banana Chalice,* which will be finished in fifteen years.

Brief Contents

Contents in Detail

Acknowledgments

Thanks to Hax for making these books happen and to Caitlin for all she had to put up with. And to my perfect nebling Camilla Grace, for giving me a material reason to want these books in the world.

Everyone Makes Games

Video games can be playful, weird, exciting, curious, magical, and even downright scary. We enjoy playing games because they act like windows into other worlds, worlds that move and change as we play with them, worlds whose rules are different than our own. (Sometimes these rules seem to make more sense than ours.) Games can be places we visit for a short time or places we get lost in for long stretches at a time. Through games, we can try on other personas and explore different perspectives.

Whatever games might mean to you, you should know that you can make your own games. And it's a lot easier than you think! The *Make Your Own Video Games* series shows you how to make fun, interactive games from scratch using a few tools.

What You'll Need

To create the games in this series, you'll need the following:

- Access to a computer
- An internet connection

That's it! In this book, we'll work with a free online tool called *Twine*, which is designed for writing branching stories similar to a *Choose Your Own Adventure* book. But you'll learn to make your Twine games do things a *Choose Your Own Adventure* book simply couldn't do!

Before you learn how to download Twine and begin making your games, let's first explore some history behind the games you enjoy today.

A Brief History of Games

Games have been around *forever*, or at least since the start of civilization. In fact, our oldest ancestors made their own games from sheep's bones (the very first dice!). They used seeds and some holes in the dirt to make the game we now call Mancala. Tic-tac-toe was first played more than 3,000 years ago in Egypt!

Games existed long before activities such as writing, painting, and 3D movies. It seems like people were born to *play*. Whenever a group of people agrees to play by a certain set of rules, a new game is born. As these games pass on to new players, the new group puts its own unique spin on it. For example, a tag player might wonder, "Wouldn't tag be more exciting if you could *rescue* people who've been tagged?" And just like that, a new rule is born: games grow and change over time like weird plants.

Games that are designed by a group of people instead of just one person are called *folk games*. No one person invented tag. More likely, tag had a million different authors who each added their own little touches. This is why so many different versions of tag, like flashlight tag, freeze tag, and kick the can, exist today. All it took was someone to come up with another, more fun way to play the game, and the rest was history.

The mobile games on your phones are *designer games*, which were made by a single person or a team of people. They aren't folk games, but they're still the result of people playing games and trying to come up with different ways to improve a game or create new games using their imagination.

While playing a game, have you ever thought, "This game would be so much cooler if it just had *this*?" If so, you have the makings of a great game designer.

Who Makes Video Games?

In the 1960s, computers were the size of an *entire room*: these huge computers were called *mainframes*. Because computers were so expensive and complicated, only a few people could use them to make video games.

One of the oldest video games, *Spacewar*, was written by punching holes into paper cards and then putting the cards into a computer. After writing out the code on paper, you then had to figure out which holes to punch on a card so the computer could read and understand the cards.

If any of the holes were wrong, you had to start over and repunch all the cards!

As you can imagine, computers were very tricky to use back then. They were also so big and expensive that only schools could afford them. In fact, most of the video games made in the 1960s and 1970s were designed by students at universities, such as the Massachusetts Institute of Technology (MIT).

But these students were not being taught game design. They were being taught serious computer programming. However, between classes, they snuck away to the computer labs and figured out how to make video games because they thought games were cool. They disguised their games as Serious Computer Programs, because the administrators would delete any programs that looked like games, calling them a waste of space.

Today, we remember all those early games but not many of the Serious Computer Programs. Keep that idea in mind if someone complains about how much time you spend making games. People might forget the serious programs, but they'll usually play a fun game for a very long time.

Computers have changed a lot since the 1960s. Now you carry around a pocket-sized computer—your smartphone—which can do so much more than a huge mainframe computer ever could and is much faster. These portable computers are also less expensive and easier to use.

In this book, you'll learn how easy it is to make your own video games using free, simple tools like Twine, which hundreds of people have used: these are people of different colors and genders, young and old. People who are sick and people who are well, those who have gone to college and those who haven't. People who like cats, people who like dogs, and those who like both. All kinds of people.

So the answer to the question *Who makes videogames?* is *everyone*!

Why Make a Video Game?

People create video games for many different reasons! For example, maybe you've tried drawing comics and it was fun. Maybe you've tried writing stories and that was fun, too. Perhaps you enjoy arts and crafts as well as making music. Odds are, if you're creative, you'll also enjoy making games.

Another reason to create games is that you really like them and want to learn how they work. Making your own games is the best way to understand how game designers make decisions when they create your favorite games.

If you don't like games very much, that's okay too! Perhaps you can make a new type of game no one has ever seen before—a game that is totally different from the currently available games. Gamers need challenges.

If you know you want to be a game developer, you could try to make games that kids will love to play for generations, which will inspire *them* wto make games.

For me, making games is exciting and new, even after all the time I've spent on them. Whenever I think I'm done, a new idea pops into my head. I can't stop thinking about it until it's out of my head, which means I have to make the idea a reality. When I create a new game, I'm creating something I can share with the world. It feels awesome!

There are tons of reasons to make a game, and they're all great reasons as long as they excite you.

What Should My Game Be About?

Games can be about *anything*. Really, it's true. They can be about big things, small things, important things, silly things, people and places, your mom or dad, a brother or sister, or your cat or dog.

They can be about things that happened to you or things you *wish* had happened to you. You could make a game about your weird dreams, about a funny story you heard, or about robots taking over the Earth.

Or perhaps your game can be about the network of secret tunnels leading from your basement to the center of the Earth (you know about those, right?) and the monsters that live in them.

You could just try re-creating games that you already play and like. Make your *own* game about the dude in the funny overalls with the mustache (Mario). For example, what would Mario do on his day off? Would he go on a picnic? Do you think he has a cat?

Although there are already games about almost everything, there is *always* room for more ideas. Don't let anyone tell you otherwise!

About Twine

Twine is all about storytelling. In fact, writing a Twine game is a lot like writing a story except the story changes in different ways—or *branches*—depending on the decisions a player makes.

How Twine Works

When you're browsing a website, you'll often see underlined text in different colors. When you click the text, an entirely new page appears. Those highlighted words are *hyperlinks*. When you combine a whole bunch of hyperlinks, you get *hypertext*. *Hyper* means that you almost instantaneously arrive at a new page that could be hundreds of light-years away.

As you'll see, Twine is like a digital version of the *Choose Your Own Adventure* book series: every hyperlink you click is a decision that takes you down a different path in the story. In Chapter 1, you'll learn how to use hypertext to create games with Twine.

Do I Need to Know How to Program?

No, you don't need to know how to program to start using Twine. As long as you know how to type words into a computer, you're ready to go! Twine has a system called *hooks* that lets you change the appearance of your story or secretly keep track of what a player has done. But you don't have to worry about either unless you want to.

What If I Don't Like to Write?

Have you ever written a story? I mean, have you written for *yourself*, not for a class? When you're making a game, you don't need to worry about what others think of it. You're making it for *you*. It can be very empowering and satisfying to work on something that's what you want it to be, free from anyone else's judgment. Writing can be like that too. If you've only ever written for other people, try writing for you before you make up your mind.

How Much Does It Cost?

Twine is free! Making your game, publishing your game, and putting your game online where other people can play it don't cost a thing! (Of course, someone in your home needs to pay for internet access, or you can try using a computer at your school or library.)

Alternative Tools

If you don't like Twine, check out the two other books in this series: *Make Your Own Video Games with Scratch* and *Make Your Own Video Games with PuzzleScript*. Unlike Twine, Scratch and PuzzleScript let you make *graphical* games, not text games.

But you should try to learn Twine, too! The more tools you know how to work with, the more versatile you'll be as a creator. The best artists can pick up and use any tool to craft something that matches their vision.

Let's get started!

1

Interview with a Cat: Twine Basics

In this chapter, we'll explore a Twine game I made called *Interview with a Cat!* To create this game, I asked my cat Encyclopedia Frown a bunch of questions, and then wrote down all of her responses. She's a very talkative kitty, and she had a lot to say!

Interview with a Cat! is a simple game in which you choose a question, Encyclopedia Frown answers it, and then you choose another question. Which question you ask next depends on Encyclopedia Frown's response to the previous question, just like in a normal conversation. For example, if she mentions her mom—that's me!—you can ask her about her mom. You'll also see pictures of my cat in this game. Sometimes she makes funny faces when you ask her certain questions. Play the game now at *https://nostarch.com/twinegames/*, and then come back when you're done.

Getting Started with Twine

Twine games are made up of words, hyperlinks, and sometimes pictures. Of course, they're not all about cats. There's no *official* rule that says they have to be. For your first game, it's best to start with a small idea. The reason is that big ideas grow like towering castles: they're beautiful, but rarely do they get finished.

Decide on an idea. It doesn't have to be the best one. You'll always have more ideas, and you can always make more Twine games, so don't worry about the game being perfect. When you have a seed of an idea, navigate to Twine's home page at *http://www.twinery.org/*. The Twine web page looks like a big pinboard with lots of little notes pinned to it.

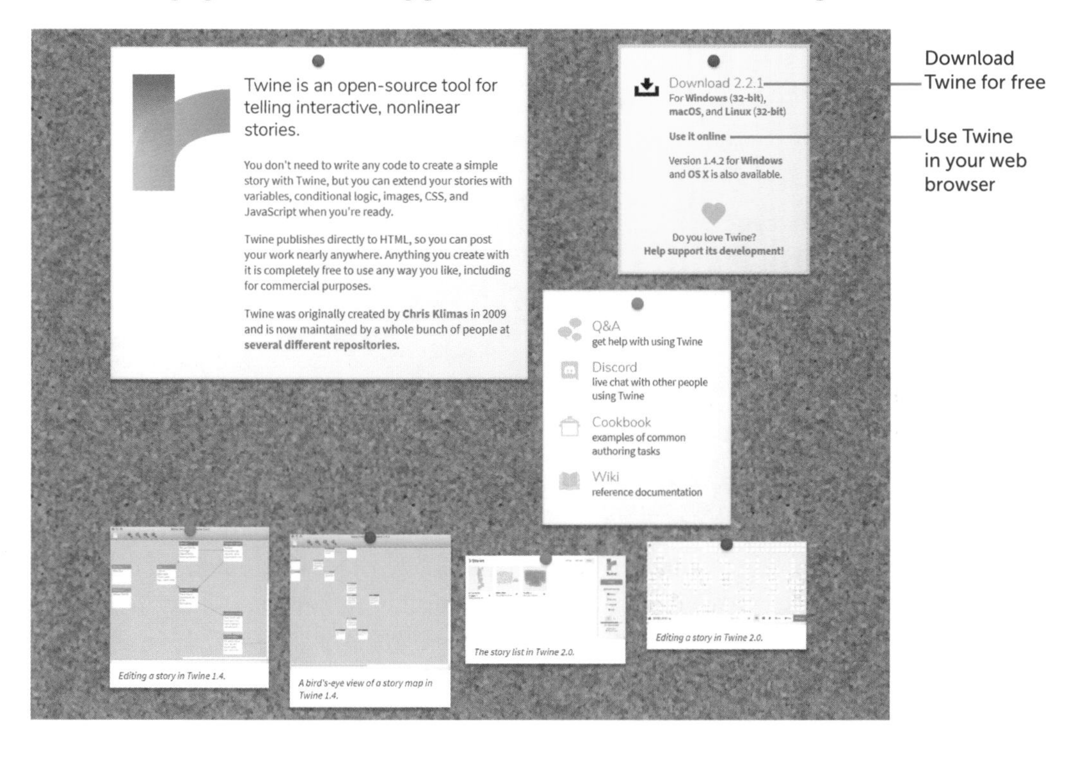

For now, we'll use Twine online so no setup is needed, and there's nothing to install:

1. Click **Use it Online**. You might see some helpful messages about Twine and some links to more information about using it. When you've finished reading those messages, you'll end up in your personal Twine library, like the one shown in the following figure. You should see a big, empty white page because you haven't written anything yet. Soon this page will be filled with all your stories!

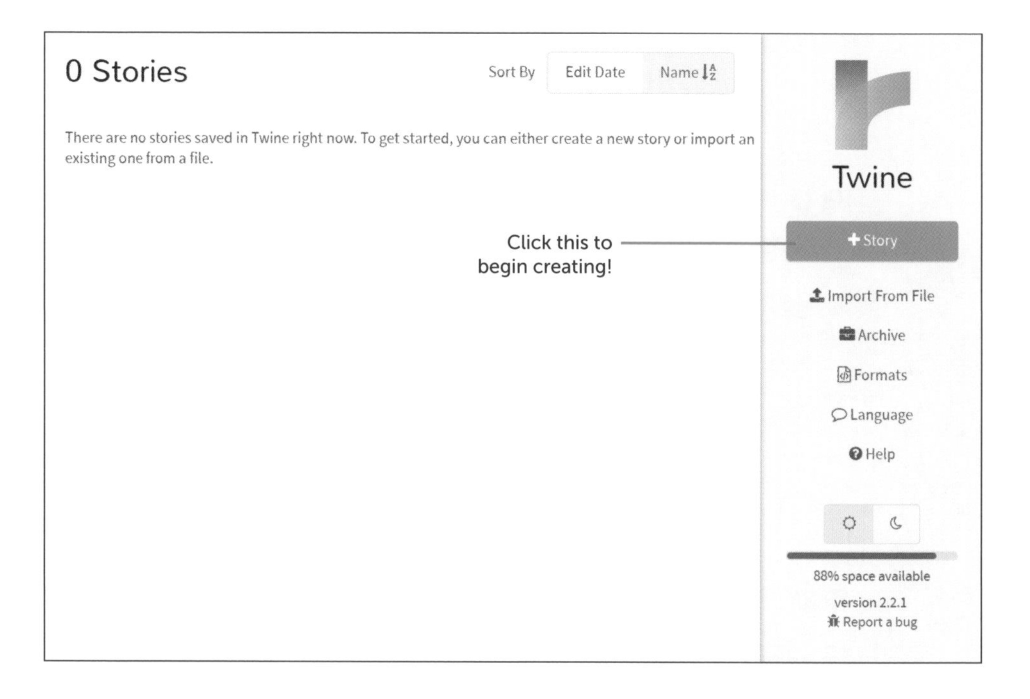

2 Click the **+Story** button. A window should pop up and ask you to name your story. For example, if you're writing about an interview with your cat Marshmallow, enter something like *The Marshmallow Interview* or *Marshmallow: The Interview*. If you want to write about an interview with your fish, your dog, an imaginary alien, or something else, write that! If you can't think of any ideas, just copy my game for now. You can always change it later.

3. After you've entered a name, click **+Add**. You should see a blue screen like this.

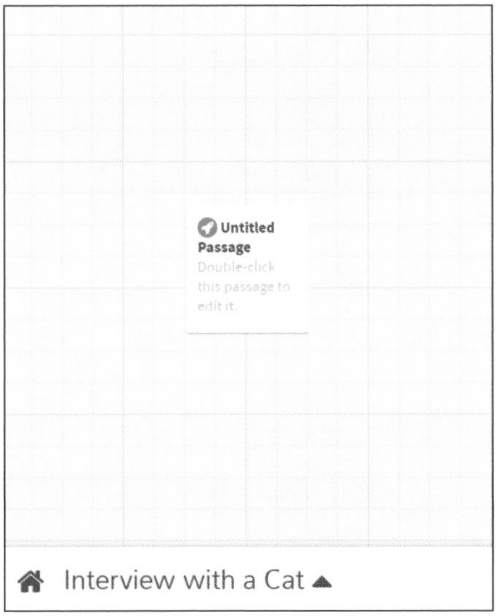

Untitled Passage
Double-click this passage to edit it.
Interview with a Cat

This is where your story will be! Right now, it's just an empty grid waiting for all your cool ideas.

Editing Passages

Think of the big blue grid like the blueprint for a house (or a castle, or an underwater laboratory, or a giant mechanical dinosaur—whatever you want). You'll add passages to this grid. A *passage* is a piece of text, but you can also think of it as a single page in your story or a single room in your blueprint.

Right now, there's only one passage, which is called *Untitled Passage* because you haven't named it yet. Double-click where it says *Double-click this passage to edit it*.

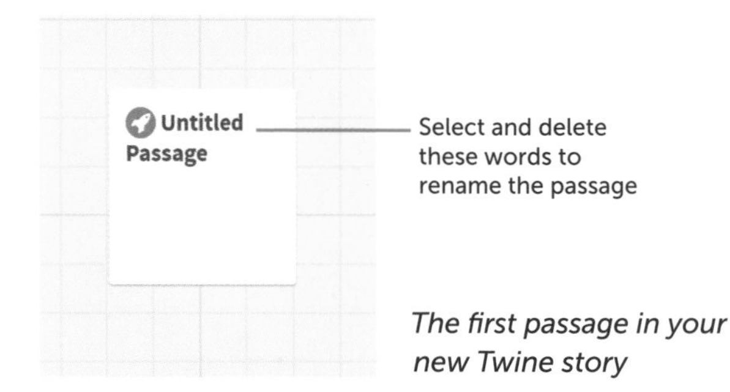

The first passage in your new Twine story

A window opens that lets you enter text. Change the name of the passage by highlighting *Untitled Passage* and pressing the BACKSPACE key to delete it.

Name this first passage **Start** because it's where the player will start.

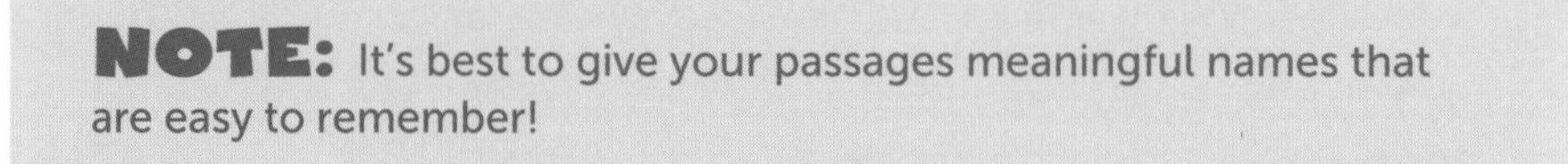

NOTE: It's best to give your passages meaningful names that are easy to remember!

Next, write the text the player will see in your game! Highlight the existing *Double-click this passage to edit it.* message and press BACKSPACE to delete it. Then a whole bunch of ghostly text will appear in the window!

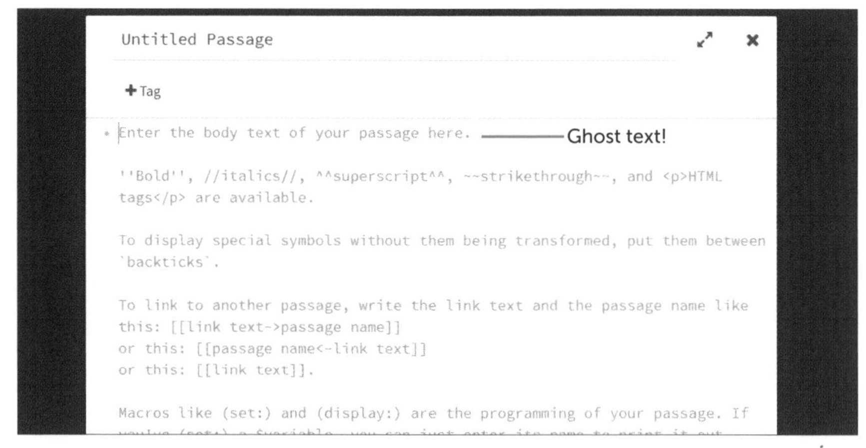

Ghostly reminder text reminds you what to write

This ghost text just reminds you how Twine works. It vanishes as soon as you start entering text. Enter the first word of my *Interview with a Cat!* game, which is `meh!`

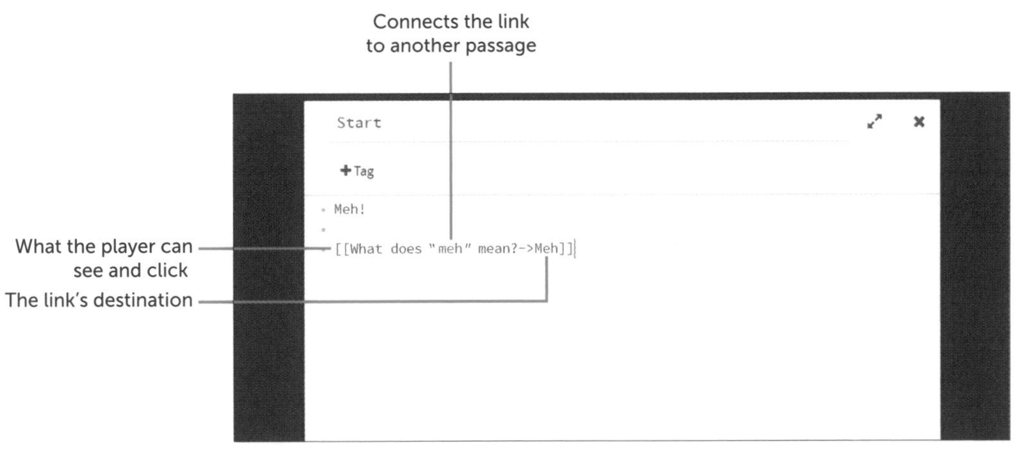

Creating links

The words in blue under `Meh!` make up a *link*, which the player clicks to go from passage to passage. Let's walk through the parts of the following link:

```
[[What does "meh" mean?->Meh]]
```

It's important to use two brackets, `[[ ]]`, on either side of the text to enclose the link. This lets Twine know that the text inside the brackets is a link and everything outside isn't. If you're not careful, you could end up selecting an entire screen as a link instead of just a few words.

The words before the arrow (`What does "meh" mean?`) are the only part the player will see. Refer back to the first figure in this chapter to see what this link looks like in a finished game. When the player clicks those words, they'll go somewhere new! But where?

That's the arrow's (->) job. It's made of a dash (-) and a greater than sign (>). The arrow connects the words in the link to the link's destination.

The third item is the link's destination. In this case, `->Meh` means the link goes to a passage called *Meh* where Encyclopedia Frown explains what "meh" means.

NOTE: From left to right, a link has the following format:

```
[[text to display in link->link destination]]
```

You can make your link the first question the player might ask your cat, dog, or alien monster. Enter what the player will see first, an arrow `->`, and then the name of the passage to link to (where the player goes). Finally, enclose everything with closing double brackets. When you're done, click the X in the top-right corner of the window to close it.

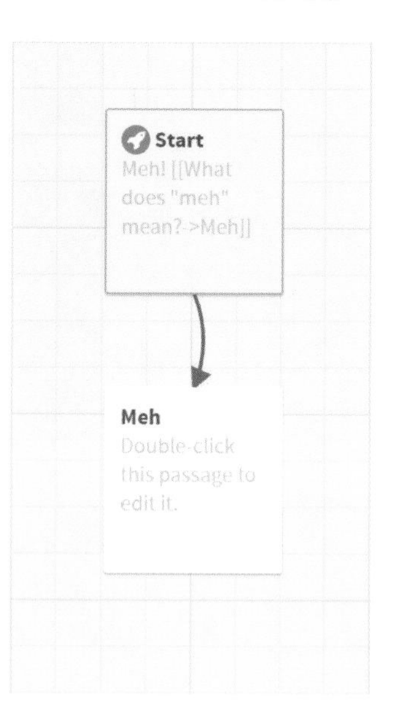

A new room should be added to your blueprint, and your screen should look something like what's shown at right.

Whenever you add links to passages, like we just did with *Meh*, Twine automatically creates those new passages for you to fill in and then saves your work.

It's best to finish writing a passage before you start filling in the new passages your links create. Let's add two more links to the *Start* passage, like this:

```
Meh!
[[Hello!->Hello]]
[[Merrow!->Cattalk]]
[[What does "meh" mean?->Meh]]
```

Close the window and presto!

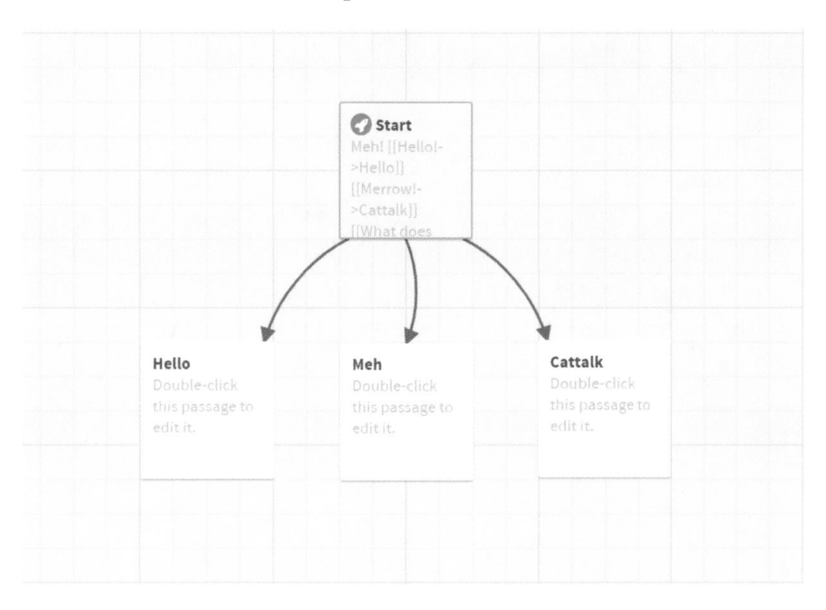

By adding links to different passages like this, you create new choices the player can explore when they play the game.

Creating Multiple Paths

Players of the *Interview with a Cat!* game can reach the same passages in multiple ways. For example, the first passage has three choices: *Hello*, *Meh*, and *Cattalk*. Each passage leads players to a different passage. But all three will eventually take the player to the same place: a main *Interview* passage with lots of different questions. This is the center of the story and is similar to a table of contents. Like a table of contents, it shows many different places the story can go, and you can always return to it to go somewhere else.

In the following figure, arrows point from the *Start* passage to lots of other passages, showing different links the player can click.

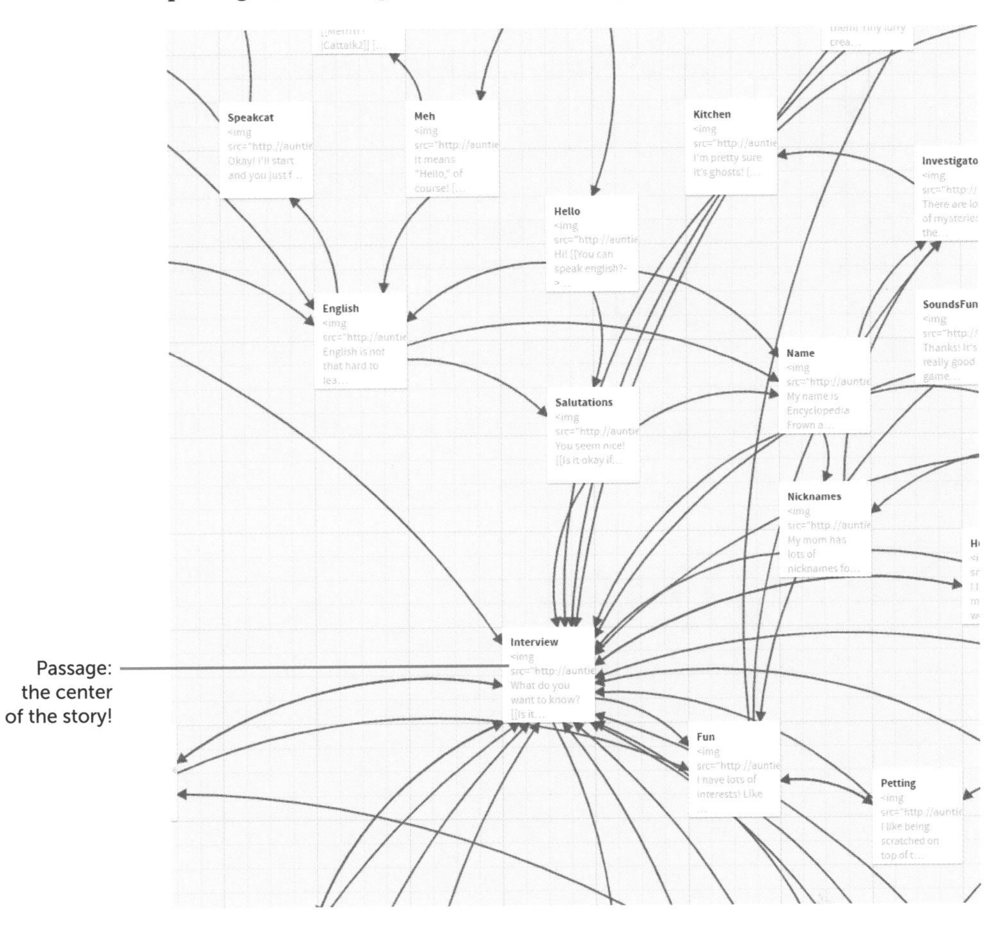

All the links lead to the *Interview* passage eventually, and so do a lot of arrows from other passages on other parts of the blueprint! As a result, the player can choose one option without being afraid that they'll miss another part of the story.

Secrets and Rewards!

You can use little prizes to motivate the player to explore your story thoroughly. For example, I use special pictures of Encyclopedia Frown in *Interview with a Cat!* as rewards for finding certain passages. In the game is a very cute photo of Encyclopedia making a face that looks like this: O_o. This photo appears in only one passage in the entire game. Did you find it? To see this photo, you have to ask Encyclopedia "one more question" and then say something that's not a question!

One cool thing about writing interactive stories is that every player's path through the game will be a little different. Try filling your games with lots of neat secrets for players to find and share with each other.

Deleting Passages

When you drag your mouse over any passage, you should see a bubble with four icons that look like a trash can, a pencil, a play button, and three dots. Let's explore what these do.

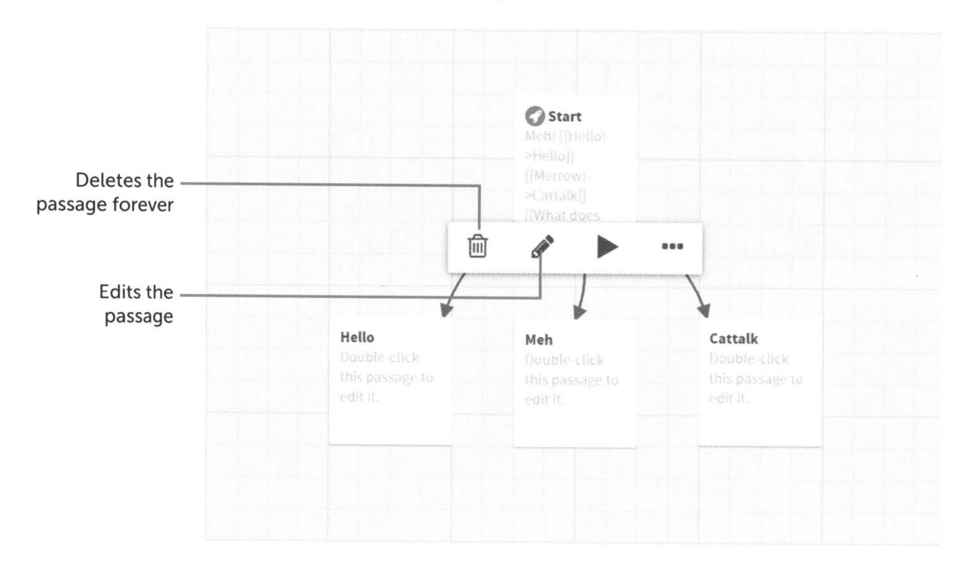

You can use the *trash can* to delete the passage, erasing it from your story *forever!* (When you click it, a warning message appears to prevent you from deleting text by accident.) The *pencil* lets you edit the passage: you can also edit it by double-clicking on the passage.

Testing Your Game

To make sure your links work the way you want them to, you can test them. The *play button* lets you test your game, beginning with the passage the bubble is pointing at. When you click it, you enter **Debug View**.

People call problems in their games *bugs*. Think of a mean little bug crawling around inside your computer pressing all the wrong buttons and messing up everything. Yuck! A bug might be that you directed a link to the wrong place or made some other error. The only way to find the bugs in your games and get rid of them is to test your game. It's a good idea to test your game every so often, just to make sure everything works correctly.

Hover your mouse over the *Start* passage and click the play button. A screen appears that looks like this.

Meh!

Hello!
Merrow!
What does "meh" mean?

Debug View

Now you can do a test run of your game. When you click your links in Debug Mode, you'll see an option to fix errors by clicking *Double-click this passage to edit it*. You should also see a small back arrow on the left.

Click the back arrow to return to the previous passage and make a different choice.

Click the back arrow to go back and make a different choice so you can test different paths. (The **Debug View** button in the corner shows additional information about your links that players won't see, such as which passage each link goes to.) When you've checked that all your links work, close the browser tab to return to Twine.

Setting the Start Passage

In the *Start* passage, you'll see a small, green rocket ship icon, which means it's the first page. To start at another passage, click "More passage options" on the bar and then click "Start Story Here" in the drop-down menu to make that passage the starting passage. The green rocket ship icon should appear on the new Start passage.

Click the **Play** button in the lower-right corner of Twine. Your game should start at the passage with the green rocket ship. Now you're playing the game the way a player would see it.

Sharing Your Twine Game

When you've finished creating your Twine game, share it with your friends and put it online, just like a game developer would do. Rad!

Follow these steps to share your game:

1. Click the name of your game on the bottom of Twine's grid screen. A menu of options pops up.

2. Click **Publish to File**. If your browser asks, click **Save File** to save your game to your computer as an HTML file, which is essentially

a web page. Your game should be in the *Downloads* folder on your machine or wherever you save downloaded files from your web browser. It'll be named something like *interview-with-a-cat.html.*

3. To share your game with someone else, just email the HTML file to them. When they receive the file, they need to open it in their web browser to play the game.

When your game is ready for prime time, you can upload it to the internet so anyone can play it. A few sites on the internet allow you to upload your game for free.

Uploading Your Game Online

The free Twine hosting site *http://philome.la* is one option for your game. It's very easy to use, but you must have a Twitter account to upload your HTML file.

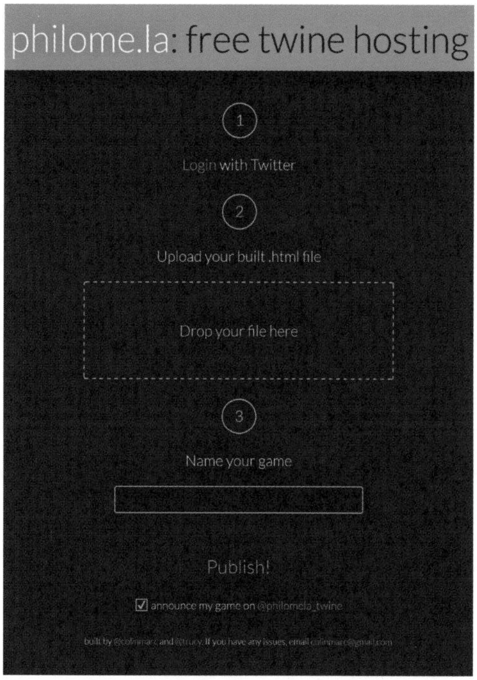

Another option is *http://textadventures.co.uk*. You don't need a Twitter account, but you'll need to register for an account at the site.

Still another option is *https://neocities.org*. Setting it up is a bit more work than on the other sites, but you can get a cool website for your game with an easy-to-remember URL. Just register a website there, such as *my-cool-game.neocities.org* (or whatever cool name is available), and upload your HTML file, like so:

1. Find your file on your computer. Its name should be something like *<Your-Game>.html*. Rename it *index.html*.
2. Fill out the information on the front page of the website, and click **Register**.
3. Click **Edit Site**, which takes you to a new page.
4. Click **Upload**. A window appears to help you select the file to upload. Choose your *index.html* file and click **Open**.

Now your game should be on the internet! Visit your brand-new website and make sure your game works.

What You Learned

Good work! Now you know the basics of using Twine. You can write passages and create links to give your player choices. You know how to test your game to make sure it's working. And you know how to export your game, share it with other people, and put it online.

But there's so much more you can do with Twine! In the next chapter, you'll learn some fun tricks to make your Twine games more expressive. You'll also use links in different ways to shape the feeling and flow of your stories. See you there!

2

Spider Milk: Weaving a Story with Links

Now that you know the basics of what Twine can do, let's talk about how to use the tools we have to really tell interesting stories! We'll look at different ways to use links, and think about how to shape our stories. We'll also go over how to make our game look more distinct with images and fancy formatting. Then we'll publish our first game!

Let's start with *Spider Milk*, a short game about visiting a monster that lives under your bed. Play along at *https://nostarch.com/twinegames/*.

Using Links

In Twine games, you can use links to influence how a player thinks about and uses them in your game. Lists of links are like different choices, similar to a restaurant menu. Every decision you make affects how the player understands your game, even if it's as simple as where you place your links and what they say.

You can also use links to shape your story in different ways. Although the player can't see your game's entire blueprint the way you can, players experience your story differently based on the shape of your game. For example, a sequence of short passages with one or two links each feels fast: *bang, bang, bang!* In contrast, a long passage bristling with lots of different links encourages the player to linger because there are so many details to take in!

Making a Choice

In many Twine games, people write their links in a list at the bottom of the passage, just as I did in *Interview with a Cat!* This approach works well in an interview game: my cat says something, you pick a question, she answers, and you pick another question.

Using a link list is best in situations in which you ask the player to choose either one thing or the other. For example, the player might need to decide whether to ride a magic dragon or a magic fruit bat, but they can't ride both. By listing the choices side by side, you invite the player to compare them and decide.

As another example, let's say you're drinking tea with the monster under your bed, as in *Spider Milk*, and the monster offers you some spider milk. You could emphasize the choice by placing the links at the bottom of the passage, as shown here.

> "Milking a spider can be tricky, but believe me, it's worth it." She offers you a small pitcher of spider milk to add to your tea.
>
> **Mix some spider milk into your tea**
> **Politely decline the offer**

Putting links at the bottom of a passage nudges the player to make a choice. They read through the entire passage, and when they reach the link list at the bottom, they choose an action.

By setting all the options together in a single list, the player can more easily see how their choices will have different consequences.

Exploring a Space

You can also use links throughout your passages to describe the player's environment. For example, here's a description of the monster's home in *Spider Milk*.

> You look around the monster's parlor. It's one of the fanciest rooms you've ever been in. A huge **chandelier** tinkles over your head. The **pillows** on the couches are all embroidered with very finely detailed pictures of monsters playing water polo. And huge, beautiful **candles** in all colors and sizes are twinkling in every corner of the room.
>
> You can't believe all of this was under your bed.
>
> "Are you going to drink your **tea** before it gets cold?" asks the monster with a smile.

In this passage, the links are objects the players notice as they look around the room. When you place links in the middle of a paragraph, you show the player what to explore, such as the *chandelier* in *Spider Milk*.

For example, clicking **chandelier** shows the player a chandelier and a single *Back* link at the bottom of the page. The *Back* link takes the player back to the previous passage so they can click *pillows* or *candles*, or just finish their tea. These extra details make your game more fun and engaging.

You look around the monster's parlor. It's one of the fanciest rooms you've ever been in. A huge **chandelier** tinkles over your head. The **pillows** on the couches are all embroidered with very finely detailed pictures of monsters playing water polo. And huge, beautiful **candles** in all colors and sizes are twinkling in every corner of the room.

You can't believe all of this was under your bed.

"Are you going to drink your **tea** before it gets cold?" asks the monster with a smile.

The chandelier gleams so brightly with hanging crystals that you can barely look at it.

Hey, those aren't crystals! They're all nickels and dimes and pennies. The monster must have collected all the coins you've dropped under your bed!

Back

When the player is done looking around the monster's home, they need to decide which link to click to move the story forward.

To help the player decide how to move to the next passage, we can hint that the *tea* link is the end of this scene by setting it apart from the other links. Conversely, we place the *chandelier*, *pillows*, and *candles* links in the same paragraph to make them seem similar to each other.

The *tea* link is the only sentence in the passage that refers to time and has a sense of urgency: "Are you going to drink your tea before it gets cold?" The other links are just objects to look at, so the *tea* link invites the player to move forward.

When you're making games, think about how to present your game to affect the player's experience. Even where links appear in a passage can affect how the player makes decisions.

Arranging Your Passages

In the previous chapter, we compared the *Interview with a Cat!* game to a blueprint for a house. Houses come in all sizes: tiny ones with just a few rooms and big, luxurious mansions with patios, verandas, and secret passages—like the kind you'll buy when you're a rich and famous game designer.

As you're creating a Twine game, you can move passages around by clicking and dragging them at any time. How you arrange your passages can change the flow of your story and your perspective on it. For example, here's the blueprint from part of *Interview with a Cat!*

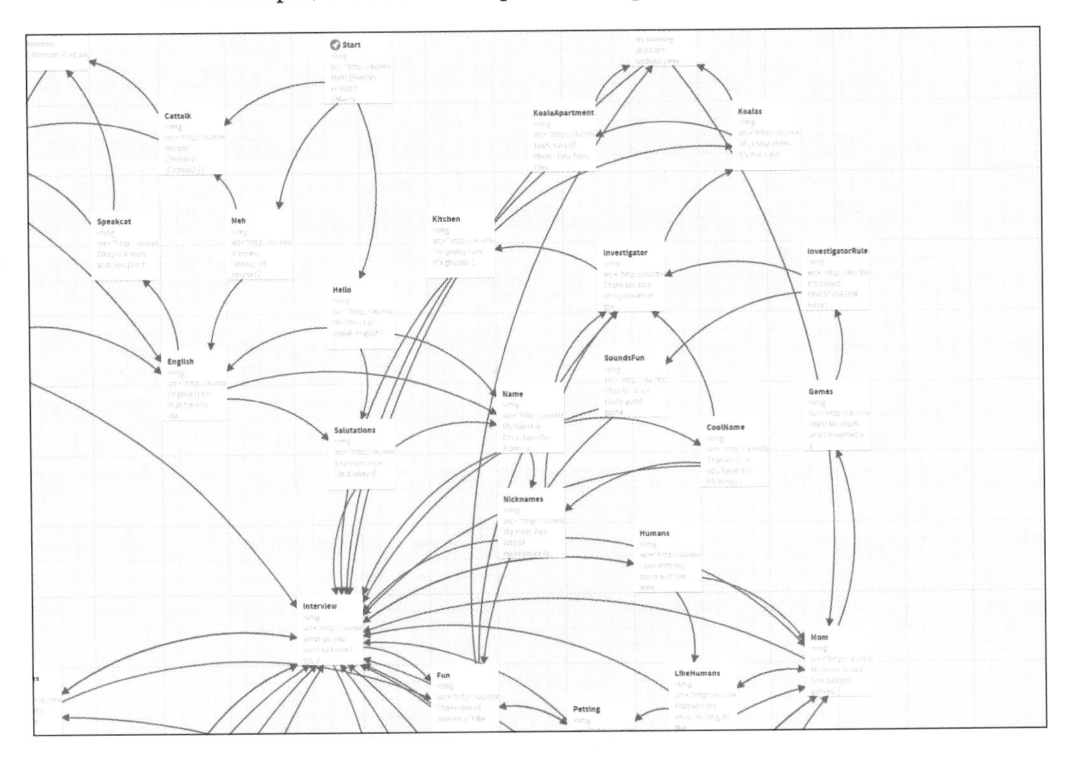

To make the interview with Encyclopedia Frown more formal, I could have lined up all the passages. But I didn't want to, because the interview is meant to be more like a friendly conversation. To create that feeling, I made the passages crisscross and connect in different ways.

When you're adding passages to your Twine games, think of your story as a house and your players as visitors. Where should your visitors go when they step into your game? How do they get around? Twine makes it easy to see your story as a map. Take advantage of this feature when you're thinking about your game's layout.

Sample Layout of a Twine Game

Let's walk through how we might think about writing a game set at a party in a mansion. Maybe the entrance to the mansion is a grand entry foyer: a big, fancy room designed to impress visitors. But there's nothing for a player to do in the foyer other than hang up their coats: it's a place of transitions.

The foyer draws the player forward toward the center of the house. They step into the main hall, another big room, full of people. A party is going on here with lots of people mingling and introducing themselves. It's loud and crowded. The player can't really get to know anyone here, but there are doors leading to smaller, more intimate side rooms.

In these side rooms, the player can stop and take in some of the details around them. They can have meaningful conversations here as well. Maybe they'll stumble upon secret passages in some of these rooms. Perhaps there's a secret door that leads from one room to another on the other side of the house or to a secret place they can't get to any other way. Maybe your player can find a little door to a backyard where they can get away from the party and look at the stars for a while. The possibilities are endless!

When your player finds their way back to the main hall eventually, perhaps many of the guests have moved to other parts of the mansion. Now they should have a better sense of the house's layout and might decide to check out another wing.

When the player decides they've seen enough, they might return to the foyer to leave the mansion. But because they've seen so many rooms in the mansion, they might think the foyer doesn't look so big and imposing anymore. Passing through the entryway on their way out, the player remembers what it looked like when they first arrived and can reflect on how their impression has changed. They retrieve their coat. It's time to go home.

Determining the Shape and Size of Your Game

Twine stories come in all shapes and sizes. Not all of them are like mansions with rooms to explore. Some are like waterfalls with only one main path, and all other paths branch off that path. Some are like gardens or caves.

When you come up with the shape of your Twine game, decide what kind of story would fit that shape. What would a robot tea party look like or a monster at the grocery store, or what happens to missing socks?

Pay attention to where paths split and then meet again. For example, some stories branch like a tree and never come back together, which means your story can have different endings. Some stories are like chain links: they come apart, come back together, come apart again, and then come back together again, creating different paths to the same ending. Others can be straight lines, and some are like meandering rivers. Try to make stories with interesting shapes, like the one shown in the following figure.

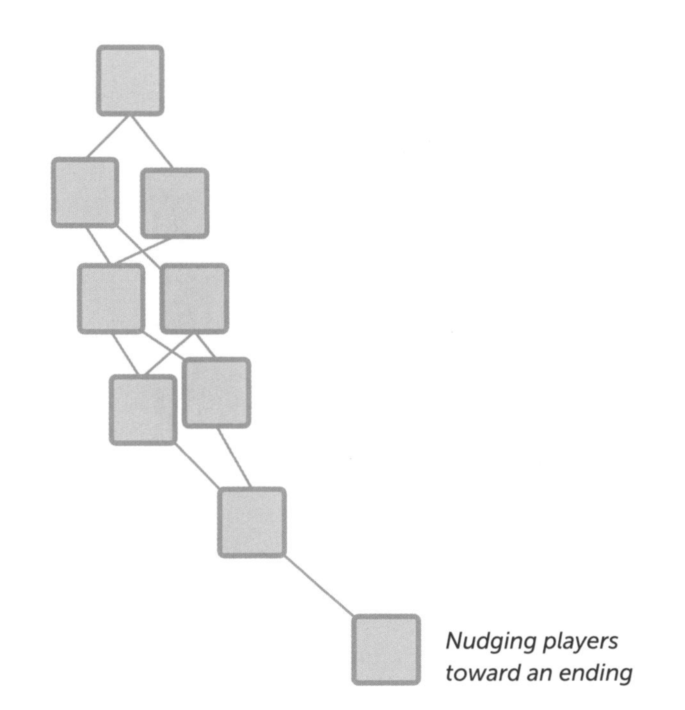
Nudging players toward an ending

Picture an action movie. The hero sees the villain on the roof of a tall building, probably laughing like a villain. We know that the scene is going to end with the hero confronting the villain, but how does the hero get there?

In our story, maybe the player chooses between running up the fire escape or taking the express elevator, but both branches lead to the exciting confrontation. Thoughtful story structuring allows us to nudge the player toward the scenes we decide are the most important, even if there are a few ways to get there.

Some Twine games are like gardens that players can wander in.

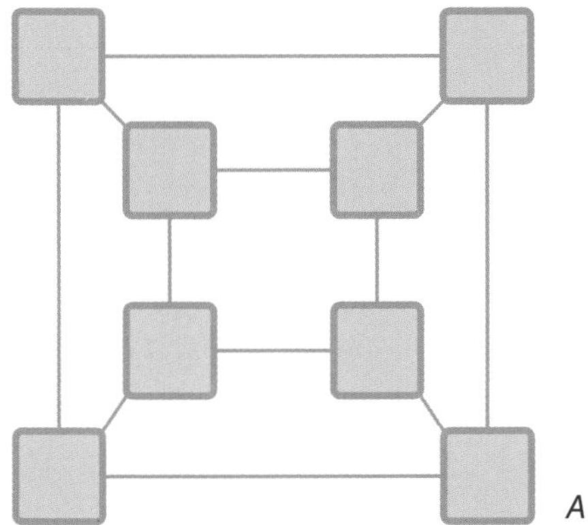
A more open-ended game

In this game shape, the player can roam through a garden looking at pretty flowers and trees, but most gardens don't have an ending. The player can leave the garden whenever they've seen enough, and maybe by the time they've walked around the entire garden, they'll feel like they know something about the person who planted it.

Some Twine games are like deep, winding caves with multiple paths that all lead to the same place.

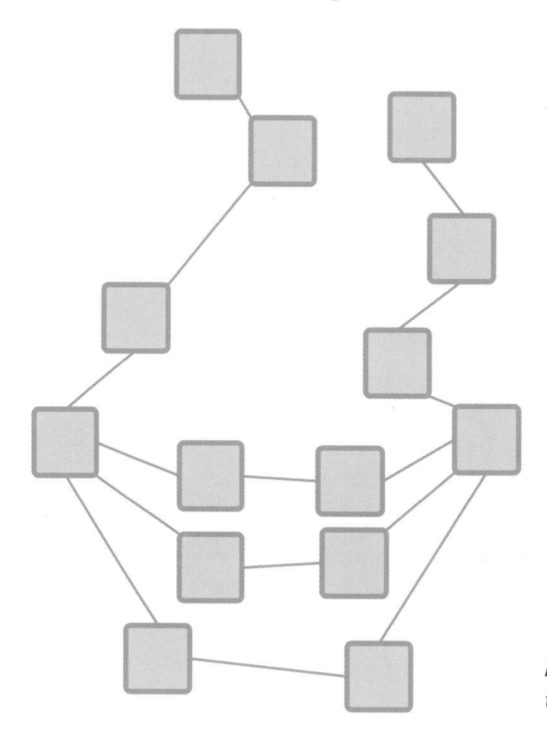

Multiple paths leading to the same place

For example, the paths in a cave can wind around and loop back in on themselves. The player can go deeper and deeper into it until they run out of light. They'll need to feel their way along the walls with their hands, not sure where they're going. They can continue down different paths until they're lost. At some point, the branches might come back together, but the player might not notice, because it's too dark. The player keeps moving forward, and when they least expect it, they see light again!

These are just some examples of different structures you can use in your games.

Emphasizing Text

You can style the words in your stories using italics, bold, or underlines to emphasize certain items or to change the way they look and feel. Let's look at how to do this.

NOTE: To learn more about ways to mark up text in your stories, view the Help option in Twine.

Italicizing

Italics are an easy way to emphasize important words in a sentence. To *italicize* text, place an asterisk (*) on either side of the text you want to italicize. For example, enter the following in Twine:

```
"I don't know about *you* but *I* like a lot of pickles on my
sandwiches. A *lot* of pickles."
```

The resulting text will look like this in your game.

"I don't know about *you* but *I* like a lot of pickles on my sandwiches. A *lot* of pickles."

Bolding

Bold text is best for headings and for important words you don't want the player to miss, like secret passwords or magic spells. Use two asterisks (**) around text you want to bold. For example, enter this in Twine:

```
**Ingredients in a Good Sandwich**
1. Lots of pickles
2. Pretty much anything else
3. Bread
**NOTE: Make sure you don't forget the pickles!**
```

Players should see this onscreen.

Ingredients in a Good Sandwich
1. Lots of pickles
2. Pretty much anything else
3. Bread
NOTE: Make sure you don't forget the pickles!

Like italics, bolding is a way to emphasize your text. Here, we used it to let the player know which words they should pay special attention to.

Underlining

You can use underlining to emphasize text, too. Enclose words in `<u>` and `</u>` to get underlined text.

The `u` means start underlining, and the `/u` means stop underlining.

Adding Pictures

At the end of *Spider Milk*, there's a little drawing of a teacup, just to put a cute little cap on the game. (I drew it in my notebook!) *Interview with a Cat!* also had pictures. You might want to use them in your games, too. Here's how to add them.

You take a sip of tea. It's kind of bland. Maybe you should have put some milk and sugar in it!

The monster sips her tea from two cups at the same time, one for each mouth. "It's so nice to get to know your neighbors," she says.

Start by uploading the image or images you want to use to the internet. One good place to do that is on *https://postimage.org/*, which lets you post images online for free. Try it now! Its home page looks like this.

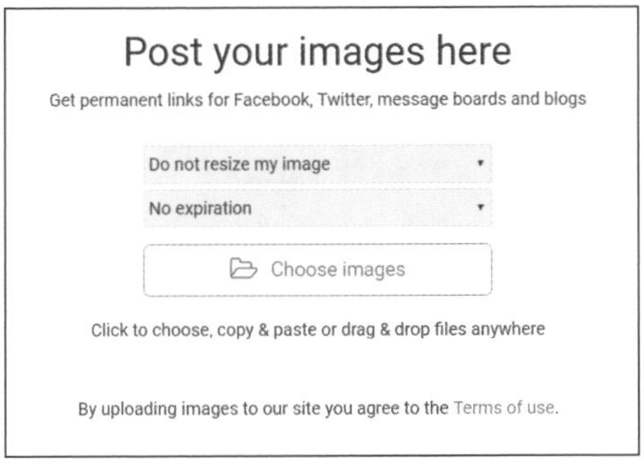

Post your images here

Get permanent links for Facebook, Twitter, message boards and blogs

Do not resize my image

No expiration

Choose images

Click to choose, copy & paste or drag & drop files anywhere

By uploading images to our site you agree to the Terms of use.

To upload a picture from your computer click **Choose images** and select the file on your computer. You can resize the image to be smaller if you want (if you don't change this option, it'll upload at its original size). The **thumbnail** and **for websites and email** sizes usually work best for Twine games.

Keep in mind that because you're uploading an image to a public site, anyone on the internet could potentially see it. They probably won't, but they *could*. So don't post anything you should keep a secret, like your address, your phone number, or the combination to your secret vault full of diamonds.

When you click **Upload It!**, your image should upload to the internet, and the following screen should appear.

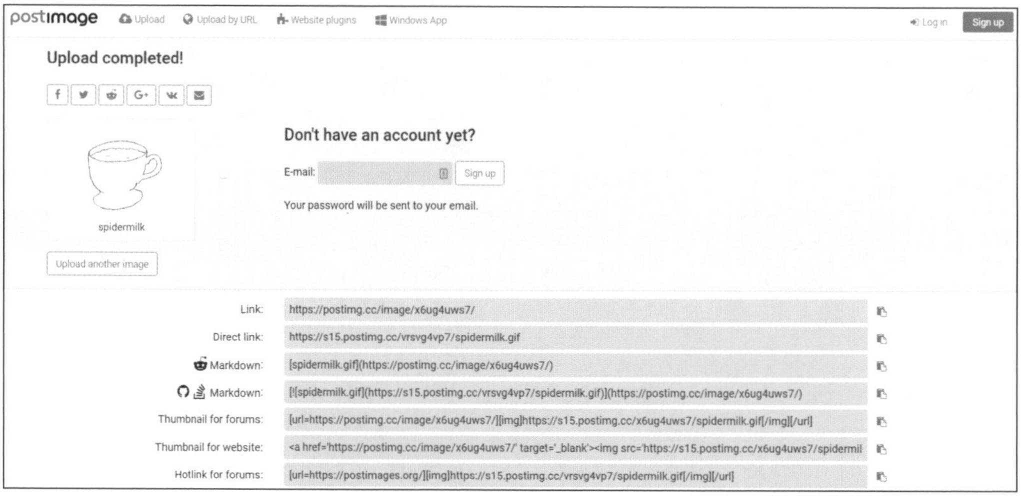

The important part of this page is the **Direct Link** option below your image. Click the **copy to clipboard** button next to the link to copy it. You can use this link to point to the image you saved to *https://postimage.org/*.

Now open the passage in your game where you want the picture to appear, and enter the following in the text of the passage:

```
<img src="
```

This tells Twine that you're adding a link to an image (`img`) and where to find the image (`src`). You have to enclose links to images in quotations, so make sure you add an opening quotation mark (`"`) before the link.

Next, right-click (or hold down the control key and click if you're using a Mac) and paste the link you copied to the clipboard previously. Close the link line using `">`. Your finished link should look something like this:

```
<img src="http://s11.postimg.org/ueht3xgsz/what.png">
```

The text inside the quotation marks is the link to the image that you uploaded.

Next, make sure your picture is embedded in your passage by clicking the play button icon in Twine. If you don't see the picture, check that you've entered the link correctly. (It might take a second for your game to load the image from the internet.)

You take a sip of tea. It's kind of bland. Maybe you should have put some milk and sugar in it!

The monster sips her tea from two cups at the same time, one for each mouth. "It's so nice to get to know your neighbors," she says.

If you see this icon, check that you pasted the correct link!

Two Versions of Twine

Twine has two different versions! We've been using Twine 2, but you can still find Twine 1 at *http://www.twinery.org/*. Unlike Twine 2, Twine 1 lets you embed images directly into your Twine games so you don't have to put them on the internet to use them. So if you're making a game with lots of images, Twine 1 might be easier to use than Twine 2. But if you're just using a few images, it's okay to stick with Twine 2.

What You Learned

In this chapter, you added a few new skills to your Twine repertoire. You explored different ways to use links to create different user experiences and different story shapes. You also learned how to italicize, bold, and underline text and how to add images to your games.

In the next chapter, you'll learn about scripting. Scripting involves writing secret words that the player won't see but will let you track what they've done and change the story accordingly. You'll also learn more ways to change what your games look like. Stay tuned!

3

Ghost Burgers: Adding Special Effects with Scripting

In this chapter, you'll learn more advanced Twine features and become a Twine virtuoso. You'll learn *scripting*, which allows you to add special effects to your story's text, and to make your game remember and respond to player choices. Now you can keep track of whether they went to one room or another or whether they're carrying a flashlight or a hamburger. You'll also learn how to change your story's background colors, font colors, and font styles. We'll use a Twine game called *Ghost Burgers* as our starting point. Play it at *https://nostarch.com/twinegames/*.

Here is what the spooky *Ghost Burgers* start screen looks like.

In *Ghost Burgers*, you explore a spooky old house to find proof of the supernatural so you and your friend Astrid can become world-famous ghost hunters. As you explore the house, you'll perform actions, like flipping a weird switch and exploring a spooky attic, to progress through the story and meet some ghosts.

Take a few minutes to play *Ghost Burgers*, and then I'll show you how to make it.

Mapping Out a Space

Unlike *Interview with a Cat!*, which simulates a conversation, *Ghost Burgers* simulates a place: a mansion. The player can move from one part of the mansion to the other and even retrace their steps to see if anything has changed in a particular room.

But before building a mansion, it's a good idea to map it out. For this game, the first step was to think about the rooms I wanted, where they were, and what events should happen in which rooms. For example, I decided the parlor would always lead to either the maintenance room or the library, and the dining room would always lead to the kitchen. This should make intuitive sense to most players. Then I drew a map like this one to help me keep track of the paths.

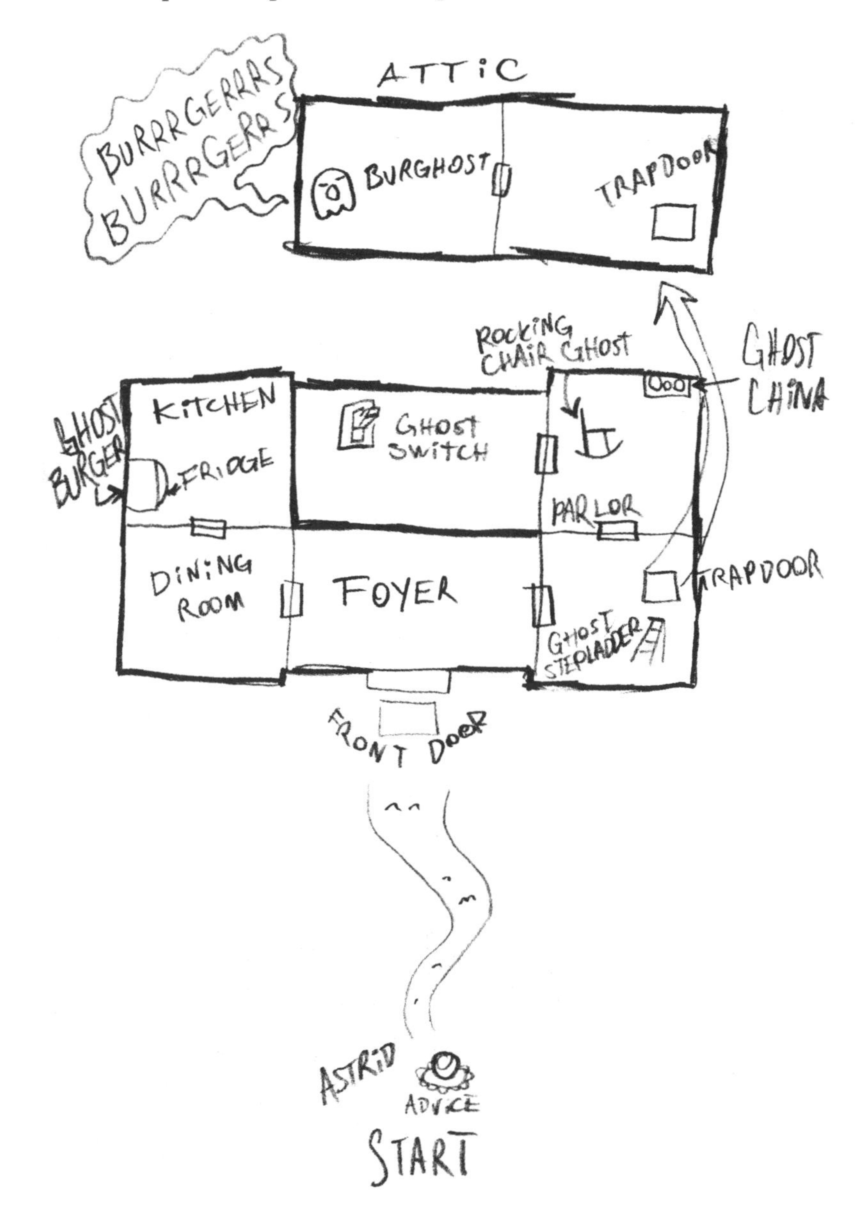

Planning Events and Controlling Play

With my map in hand and a basic idea of what the *Ghost Burgers* mansion would look like, I made a list of major events I wanted to happen in the game. The list looked something like this, in the general order in which the events would take place:

- Find a key under the doormat and use it to get into the mansion
- Discover the trapdoor that leads to the attic
- Turn on the ghost switch to make ghosts appear
- Use the ghost stepladder to reach the attic trapdoor
- Meet Burger Ghost in the attic
- Find the ghost burger in the fridge
- Find a plate of ghost china for the burger
- Feed the ghost burger to Burger Ghost

Ghost Burgers isn't super strict about the order in which these events happen. For example, the player can find the burger before meeting the Burger Ghost, or they can find the plate before finding the burger that goes on the plate. The reason to make a list of events is to have a general idea of the flow of the game.

To make your games a bit more challenging and interesting, you can make the player do things in a specific order. For example, I can make

sure the player sees the trapdoor that leads to the attic *before* the ghost stepladder appears. When the player sees the trapdoor and can't find a way up to it, they'll have to keep exploring to find out how to get up there. Later, when they flip a ghost switch, the ghostly stepladder appears, which shows the player how to access a different dimension of the game.

To ensure that the player sees the trapdoor before the ghost switch, I made it impossible for the player to get to the ghost switch without passing through the library where the trapdoor is. As you can see on the map on page 37, the player *must* pass through the library to get to the maintenance room and flip the switch. This works both ways: after the player flips the switch, they *must* pass through the library again where they'll see the ghostly stepladder.

Flipping the switch also reveals many new items for the player to explore. For example, the player can examine the fridge and the china cabinet before flipping the ghost switch, but they won't see the burger and plate until the ghost switch is on. This technique adds to the experience because the player must look around to get a sense of what's going on and anticipate changes to the game environment.

I also decided to make two of the most important moments in the game—finding the ghost burger and finding the plate to put it on—happen on opposite sides of the mansion. That way, the player has to explore the entire mansion before they can finish the game.

NOTE: Not all Twine games will have the kind of organization that *Ghost Burgers* does. Some Twine stories only move forward. But even in those stories, it's best to think about the order in which the player discovers things, what they learn and when, and where important moments in the game are in relation to each other so you can space out the game's components.

Adding Text Effects Using Hooks

The rooms in *Ghost Burgers* change from one visit to the next, but only after the player flips the switch. After the player flips the ghost switch, ghosts (like Archibald Prancibald, the talkative gentleman ghost, or the ghostly stepladder or ghost burger) appear in places that were previously ghost free! And the text looks ghostly, too!

How do you create spooky ghost text? How do you make a passage in your story look different each time the player returns to it? How do you change passages depending on what the player has already done or seen?

The answer to all these questions is to use hooks. In this chapter, I will sometimes refer to writing hooks as "script" or "code." Those are just different names for instructions that are given to a computer.

For our first hook, let's add *s p o o k y* text to our game!

Ghostly Text Style

Did you notice while playing *Ghost Burgers* that the names of ghostly objects appear ghostly, like the blurry word *stepladder* shown here?

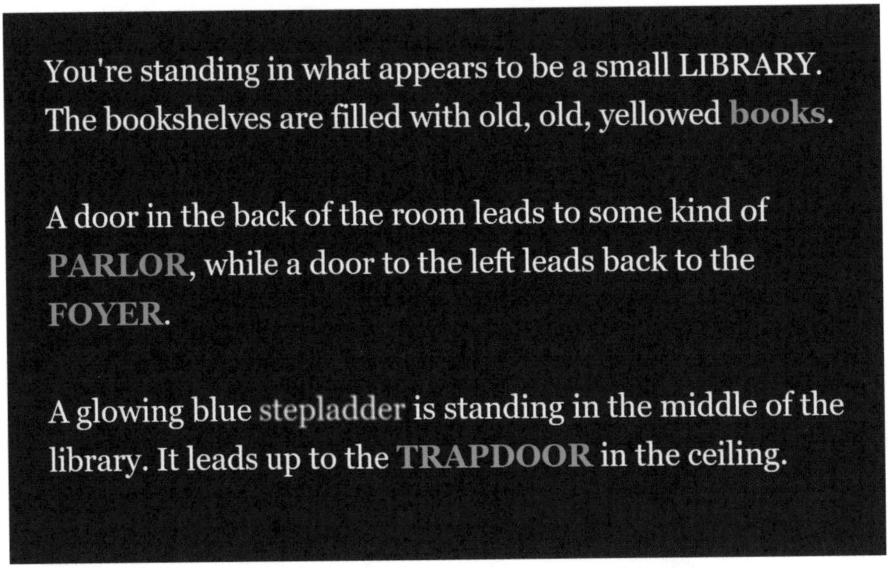

> You're standing in what appears to be a small LIBRARY. The bookshelves are filled with old, old, yellowed **books**.
>
> A door in the back of the room leads to some kind of **PARLOR**, while a door to the left leads back to the **FOYER**.
>
> A glowing blue stepladder is standing in the middle of the library. It leads up to the **TRAPDOOR** in the ceiling.

Blurring the word makes the text stand out, which helps players notice that the stepladder wasn't there the first time they traveled through this room: they would have remembered a blurry ladder! The blurry text identifies what has changed in each room.

To create these effects, you can use hooks, which are built into Twine. To see how they work, open a new passage in Twine and enter the following line into the editor:

```
A glowing blue (text-style: "blur")[stepladder] is standing
in the middle of the library.
```

Test-play this passage, and you should see that the word *stepladder* looks blurry.

In this example, the text enclosed inside parentheses `(text-style: "blur")` is the *hook*, which is a label you can use to tell Twine how to style a passage. The text in square brackets `[stepladder]` is the tagged word. Here, the `text-style` tag changes the style of the text in the square brackets from the default to the `"blur"` style. You can apply a range of styles using the `text-style` tag: for example, you can create upside-down text with `(text-style: "upside-down")` and create text that casts a shadow with `(text-style: "shadow")`. As long as you enclose the text within the square brackets, you can apply the style change to as much text as you like. (A complete list of text effects is at the Twine 2 reference site at *http://twine2.neocities.org/*.)

Displaying Random Text with either

In addition to using hooks to apply different text effects, you can also use them to display different text each time the player revisits a passage. For example, in *Ghost Burgers*, if the player looks at a book in the library more than once, they'll see a different book each time.

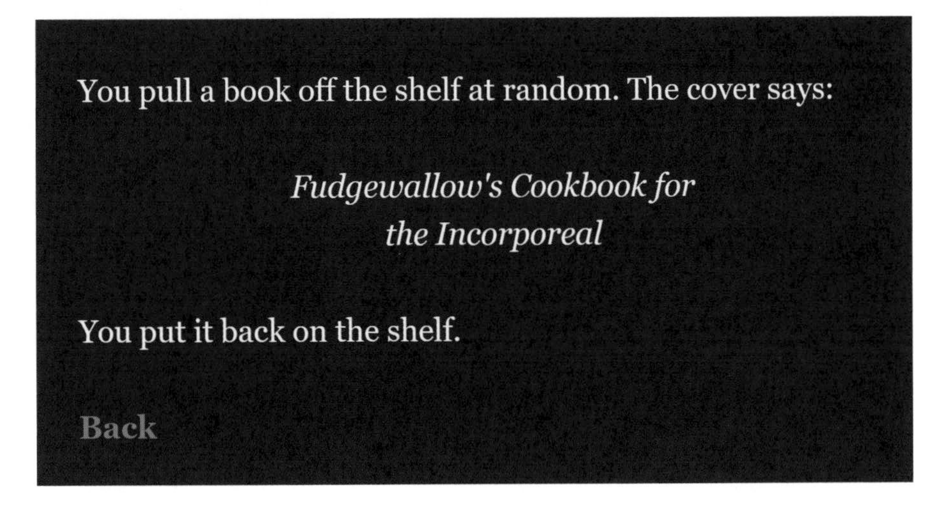

Displaying random books creates the impression of a library full of books. Almost every time the player pulls a book off the shelf, they'll see a different title. In fact, only 10 book title options are available, but that's enough to make it seem like the library has so many books the player will never be able to look at them all.

You can use Twine's `either` tag to pick from a list of options at random. For example, open a passage in Twine and enter the following:

```
(either: "red","blue","green")
```

Now test-play the passage a couple of times. The passage should read *red, blue,* or *green* each time you play it.

Each option can be as long or short as you like, but you must enclose it in quotation marks with commas between the options.

Here's how we use `either` in the *Library* passage:

```
You pull a book off the shelf at random. The cover says:
=><=
*(either: "Rotwither's Potions for Beginners", "Dead but
Not Silent: Know Your Rights", "Beyond Lydia Deetz: Can the
Living and the Dead Coexist?", "1001 New Uses for Ectoplasm",
"No More White Sheets: Fashion for the Post-Living", "This
Really Old House: Secret Passages for Cheap", "A Specter
Haunting Europe: A Travel Guide for Spirits", "Nightfallow's
Abridged Magical Grimoire", "Haunted: Learning to Let Go of
Your Past", "On Poltergeisting", "Fudgewallow's Cookbook for
the Incorporeal")*
<==
You put it back on the shelf.
[[Back->Library]]
```

The symbols =><= center the book titles, and <== moves the text back to the left afterward. To use these directional characters to format your text, enter them into Twine, and then insert the text you want to adjust on the line that follows. To move text to the right, use ==>.

The asterisks (*) at either end of the list of book title options italicize the text, as you learned in Chapter 2. When you test-run this passage, you should see something like this.

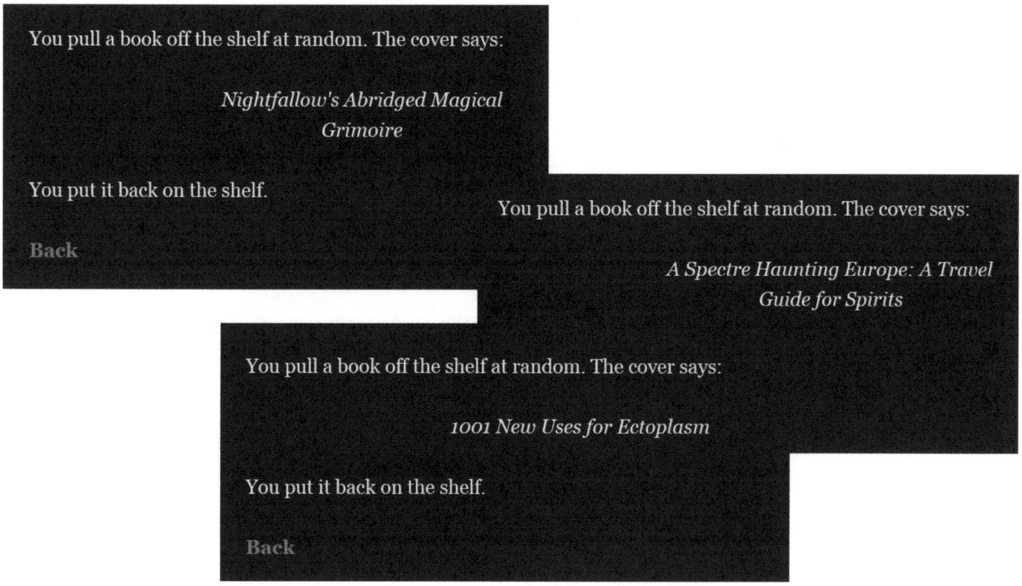

You pull a book off the shelf at random. The cover says:

Nightfallow's Abridged Magical Grimoire

You put it back on the shelf.

Back

You pull a book off the shelf at random. The cover says:

A Spectre Haunting Europe: A Travel Guide for Spirits

You pull a book off the shelf at random. The cover says:

1001 New Uses for Ectoplasm

You put it back on the shelf.

Back

Next, let's explore how to place hooks inside other hooks.

Nesting Hooks

You can combine the effects of different hooks by placing one inside the other, which is called *nesting*. Enter the following to see how nesting works:

```
(text-style: (either:"italic","shadow","blur","upside-down",
"rumble"))[What am I?]
```

Here, the words "What am I?" would randomly appear italicized, with a shadow, blurry, upside-down, or rumbling (shaking up and down). Each hook starts with text that shows what it does (`text-style`, `either`), a colon, and then a "how do I do it" part. The "how do I do it" part for the `text-style` tag is the `either` hook. We're telling Twine to print this text using either italicized, shadowed, blurry, upside-down, or rumbling style. Try it! Just make sure each hook has its own opening parenthesis and closing parenthesis!

Think of nesting hooks like nesting dolls. When you open the "text-style" doll, you'll find the "either" doll nested neatly inside it. As long as every doll has a top and a bottom—the "what do I do" and "how do I do it" with the correct punctuation—you can nest as many hooks inside other hooks as you like.

This nested tag sends the player to a random room in the mansion:

```
(display: (either:"Foyer","DiningRoom","Kitchen","Library",
"Parlor","Maintenance"))
```

Each item inside the `either` hook is the name of a passage in the game. The `either` hook is nested inside a `display` hook, which allows you to show the contents of one passage inside another. (It's more useful than you might realize!)

Using display to Avoid Retyping Text

The `display` hook can be very handy because it lets you show any passage inside any other passage. For example, say you want to display the same text (like a description of a gorgeous sunset) in a few different places. The player can see the sunset from any room in the house: through the bedroom windows or out the window in the front door. Instead of writing the description of the sunset twice, you write it once, save it as the *Sunset* passage, and then use `display` to show that passage in several rooms.

As another example, when the player talks to Archibald in *Ghost Burgers*, they'll see the same list of questions no matter which order they ask them in. After they ask a question, Archibald will answer it. Then the player can ask another one. We show the same list of questions at the end of every one of Archibald's answers, so the player can pick the next one.

We *could* retype the five questions in every passage, but if we later decide to change one of the questions or add a new one, we'd have to make the same change five times. To avoid this, we just put the questions in their own passage and use `display` to show that passage whenever Archibald is done talking, like so:

```
(display: "Archibald-Questions")
```

Now the contents of the displayed passage should appear wherever you put the `display` hook. The text of the *Archibald-Questions* passage looks like this:

```
//You say://
[["What are you reading?"->Archibald-Reading]]
[["What's it like being dead?"->Archibald-Dead]]
[["How did you die?"->Archibald-How]]
[["Are there any other ghosts here?"->Archibald-Others]]
[["Goodbye for now."->Archibald-Bye]]
```

We're writing these questions in their own passage called *Archibald-Questions.* Then we're using a hook to display the text from that passage inside another passage.

The following is what the passage looks like in the editor after the player asks Archibald how he died:

```
"I lost a staring contest against my rival," he says
seriously. "It was a very intense staring contest."
(display: "Archibald-Questions")
```

And this is what the player sees.

The `display` hook lets you reuse passages in more than one place so you don't have to do a lot of retyping.

Using Variables to Store Information

Some rooms in *Ghost Burgers* appear differently the second time a player visits them. One reason is that I use `display` to skip some of the messages in *Ghost Burgers* the second time a player visits a room. For example, the first time the player climbs the ghost stepladder, they see the *Climbing the Stepladder* passage and a message saying how weird it is that a stepladder could be a ghost. But the next time they use the stepladder, I just use `display` on the *Attic* passage so the player can skip straight to the attic.

Whether or not the player sees the *Climbing the Stepladder* passage depends on whether or not the player has already climbed the stepladder. To determine whether the player has already used the stepladder, you can use a *variable* to store information about the game play. Variables *vary*, which means the information they store can change.

Ghost Burgers uses 12 different variables. One variable keeps track of whether the front door to the mansion is locked. Other variables track whether Archibald has introduced himself to the player, whether the player is carrying the ghost burger, whether they've cleared away the cobwebs in the attic, whether their flashlight is on, and so on.

Let's look at the flashlight variable. The first time the player enters the mansion, they see a couple of sentences about turning on their flashlight.

It's pitch dark in here! You almost make up your mind to quit and leave this scary house behind forever - when you remember the flashlight in your pocket. Oh yeah.

You turn it on.

You are in a creepy cobwebbed FOYER. A huge doorway leads left to a **DINING ROOM**, while a much smaller one leads right to what looks like a **LIBRARY**.

Moonlight streaks through the open door, leading back outside to the **FRONT STOOP**.

But clearly they shouldn't see this message every time they walk through the foyer, because after the player has entered the mansion, we can assume their flashlight is still on. That's why I use the variable `$flashlight_on` to help Twine remember that the player's flashlight is on. In Twine, variable names always start with a dollar sign ($), but you can include as many as you want for free.

Boolean Variables

There are several different variable types. For example, `$flashlight_on` is a *Boolean* type. (It's named after a mathematician named George Boole.) A Boolean variable has a value of either `true` or `false`, like the switch on a flashlight. If `$flashlight_on` is `true`, the flashlight is on. If `$flashlight_on` is `false`, the flashlight is off.

After you create a Boolean variable, you can use Twine hooks to check your variables and display different text depending on the variable's value or condition. For example, when the player enters the foyer and turns on their flashlight, they shouldn't see a message about turning it on again. So, I wrote a hook to display a different message depending on the condition of the flashlight—whether it's on or off. This is called a *conditional* statement because different conditions determine which message is shown.

Conditional statements use two major hooks: `set` and `if`. You use `set` to set a variable to a value. For example, to turn on the flashlight, you set the `$flashlight_on` variable to `true`:

```
(set: $flashlight_on to true)
```

Then you can use `if` to check the variable's value.

Using if to Check a Variable's Value

In *Ghost Burgers*, we use variables to track whether the front door to the mansion is locked (`true` for yes, `false` for no), whether the player is carrying a hamburger (`true` for hamburger, `false` for no hamburger), or whether the player has turned on their flashlight.

Checking Whether the Flashlight Is On

To see if the flashlight is on, you can use `if` to check whether the `$flashlight_on` variable is `true` or `false`:

```
(if: $flashlight_on is true)
```

The following is the full code for the *Foyer* passage. It uses `set` and `if` to keep track of whether or not the flashlight is on.

```
(if: $flashlight_on is false)[It's pitch dark in here! You
almost make up your mind to quit and leave this scary house
behind forever - when you remember the flashlight in your
pocket. Oh yeah.
You turn it on. (set: $flashlight_on to true)
]You are in a creepy cobwebbed FOYER. A huge doorway leads
left to a [[DINING ROOM->Dining-Room]], while a much smaller
one leads right to what looks like a [[LIBRARY->Library]].
Moonlight streaks through the open door, leading back outside
to the [[FRONT STOOP->Doorstep]].
```

First, we use a Boolean to check whether the flashlight is off using `(if: $flashlight_on is false)`. If it's `false`, the `if` tag displays everything in the square brackets after it—the part where the player turns their flashlight on.

Then we use the conditional `set` to change the `$flashlight_on` variable from `false` to `true` using `(set: $flashlight_on to true)`, which keeps track of having shown that message. So the next time the player comes through the room, the message won't display again, because `(if: $flashlight is false)` will no longer be true.

Triggering Different Messages Based on Flashlight Condition

But let's say you want to show one message when the flashlight is on and a different message when it's off. To do so, you can use `else`:

```
(if: $flashlight_on is true)[Thank goodness your flashlight is
on!](else:)[It's pitch dark! If only your flashlight was on!]
```

To use `else`, just add `(else:)` and text in square brackets to the end of an `if` statement. If the `if` statement isn't `true`, the text inside the `else` statement displays.

Note that both hooks are on the same line because Twine detects *whitespace*—the empty spaces between paragraphs. In fact, sometimes you can accidentally introduce empty spaces into your story by pressing enter in the middle of your hooks. One solution to avoid accidentally adding whitespace is to use braces `{}` to tell Twine to display everything between the braces on one line, like this:

```
{
(if: $flashlight_on is false)[It's pitch dark in here!]
(else:)[It would be pitch dark without your flashlight on!]
}
```

Now, everything between `{` and `}` will display in your story as though it's all on one line, even though it spans several lines of code. This syntax is particularly useful when you're writing lots of hooks in your passages, because you can use whitespace to make the hooks easier for you to read without displaying the whitespace to the player.

Making Ghosts Appear Conditionally

In *Ghost Burgers*, we use `if` and `else` to determine whether ghosts should appear as shown in the Library code:

```
You're standing in what appears to be a small LIBRARY.
The bookshelves are filled with old, old, yellowed
[[books->Read-Book]].
A door in the back of the room leads to some kind of
[[PARLOR->Parlor]], and a door to the left leads back to the
[[FOYER->Foyer]].
```

```
(if: $ghosts_visible is false)[It seems like there's a
trapdoor in the ceiling, too! But it's way too high to
reach.](else:)[A glowing blue (text-style: "blur")[stepladder]
is standing in the middle of the library. It leads up to the
[[TRAPDOOR->Climb-Ladder]] in the ceiling.]
```

If ghosts aren't visible (`(if: $ghosts_visible is false)`), the player only sees the trapdoor. If ghosts are visible, we use `(else:)` to display the ghost ladder leading up to the trapdoor so the player can climb it.

> **NOTE:** A link can be part of a hook, too. Just make sure you use two square brackets on either side of a link or one on either side of the hook.

Now you know how to show items based on certain conditions.

Integer Variables

To keep track of more than two items or events, you can use an integer variable. An *integer* is a whole number that isn't a fraction, such as 1, 10, 33, 5000, or 0.

For example, in *Ghost Burgers*, the player can talk to their friend Astrid if they don't know what to do next or can't figure out something, and Astrid will give them a hint. The following figure shows an example.

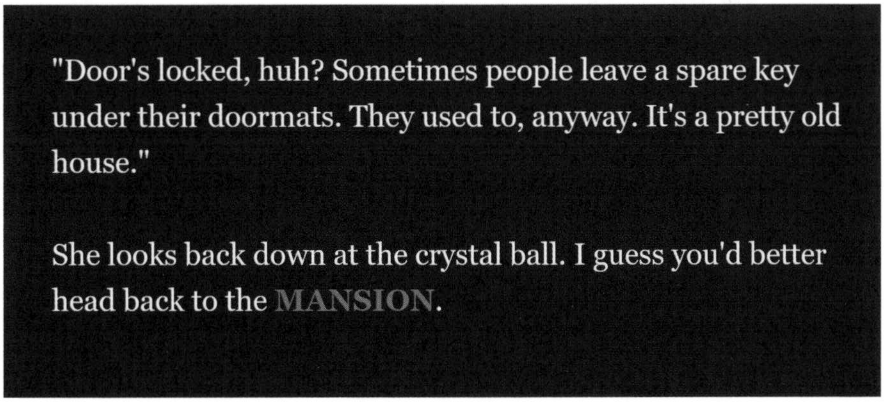

"Door's locked, huh? Sometimes people leave a spare key under their doormats. They used to, anyway. It's a pretty old house."

She looks back down at the crystal ball. I guess you'd better head back to the MANSION.

If the player talks to Astrid when they're looking for a burger, she'll give them one piece of advice. If the player already has the burger and hasn't fed it to the Burger Ghost, she'll give them a different piece of advice. In fact, the game has eight different pieces of advice. Astrid also has something special to say the first time the player consults her after turning on the ghost switch.

We use an integer variable to keep track of which piece of advice Astrid should give the player. Each number in the variable matches a different piece of advice. Here's a sample of what that code looks like:

```
{
(if: $advice is 0)["Oh, go on, it's not *that* scary. Just
try the door."]
(if: $advice is 1)["Door's locked, huh? Sometimes people
leave a spare key under their doormats. They used to, anyway.
It's a pretty old house."]
(if: $advice is 2)["Try looking around the mansion! There's
*got* to be something ghostly in there!"]
(if: $advice is 3)["Wait, you found a cool glowing switch and
you *didn't try switching it on?* What's the worst that could
happen?"]
(if: $advice is 4)["Did you try looking around the attic?
Attics in creepy old houses are *always* haunted."]
}
```

The integer variable `$advice` starts at 0. When the player discovers that the door is locked, the game sets `$advice` to 1. When the player unlocks the door, the game sets `$advice` to 2. If the player finds the ghost switch but doesn't switch it on, `$advice` is set to 3. When the player flips the switch, `$advice` is set to 4. Whenever the player talks to Astrid, the game checks all possible numbers for the `$advice` variable and shows the message that matches the number that `$advice` is currently set to.

You can set your variables to whatever you want them to start with in the first passage of your game; however, make sure the player can't return to this passage, or the game will reset all those variables to their starting positions! I set up all my variables once in the starting passage of my game. Think of it like a title screen in a movie: once the player clicks **Start**, they'll never come back to this passage.

```
(set: $advice to 0)
```

By putting this line of code in my starting passage, I make sure that the `$advice` variable is set to `0` when a player starts the game.

Ghost Burgers has 12 variables in total. Here's what the entire first passage in *Ghost Burgers* looks like. I put braces around all the variables because otherwise Twine would print an entire blank line for each one:

```
=><=
{
    (set: $advice to 0)
    (set: $door_locked to true)
    (set: $found_key to false)
    (set: $flashlight_on to false)
    (set: $ghosts_visible to false)
    (set: $climbed_ladder to false)
    (set: $ghost_lecture to false)
    (set: $archibald_intro to false)
    (set: $checked_fridge to false)
    (set: $got_china to false)
    (set: $got_burger to false)
    (set: $cleared_cobwebs to false)
}<img src="http://auntiepixelante.com/ghostburgers/
ghost_burgers.png">
[[START->Astrid-1]]
```

When the player starts the game, the door should be locked, the ladder should be unclimbed, the mysterious burger not yet collected. Because the player hasn't done anything at the beginning of the game, most of the variables start as *false*. When the player clicks **START**, all the variables should be reset, and the player should be able to play a new game!

Editing Your Story's Stylesheet

Little changes in your story's appearance can have a big effect on how a player feels while playing your game. Does *Ghost Burgers* feel spookier than *Interview with a Cat!* because it's on a black background (representing nighttime) instead of a bright white one? Do the blurry words in the story feel ghostlier than the solid words around them? Experiment with changing the appearance of your story and see if its new style changes your perspective. Your story can be as stylish as you want it to be.

Most websites use *Cascading Style Sheets (CSS)* to determine what the site looks like. Twine also uses CSS, and it's easy to change Twine's stylesheet using CSS. A *stylesheet* in Twine describes how elements on a web page should look. Twine comes with its own stylesheet that describes how Twine games should look, but you could change it to make the text blue and the background pink.

To find your story's stylesheet, click the name of your story (below the blue story grid), and then click **Edit Story Stylesheet**, as shown here.

The *Ghost Burgers* stylesheet looks like this.

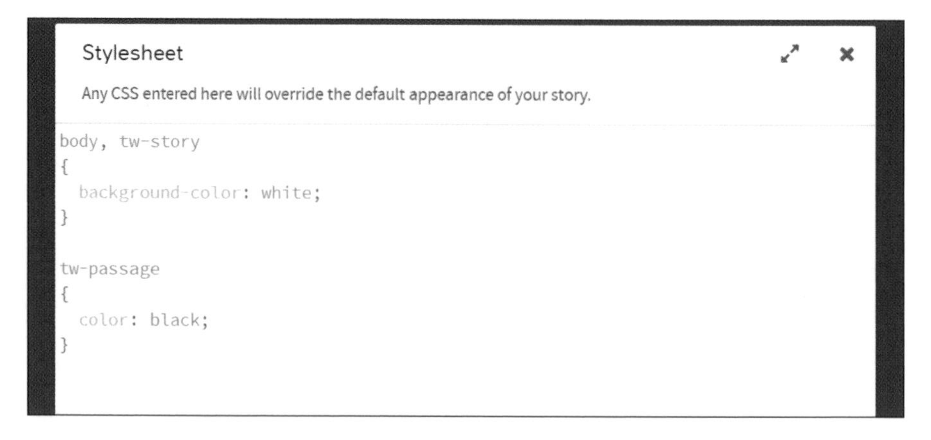

This is where you change your story's appearance. If you don't make any changes, Twine will just use the existing stylesheet. Let's look at how to make some changes.

Changing the Background Color

When you make a new Twine game, its stylesheet is blank. The first change I like to make is to modify the background color. Add this code to your Twine game's stylesheet:

```
body, tw-story
{
  background-color: black;
}
```

This code sets the page's background color to black. The `body` refers to the web page itself, and `tw-story` is short for "Twine story" and affects how your story looks. Everything between the braces, `{ }`, describes your Twine game's `body`.

When you copy this code into your story's stylesheet, make sure you enter everything precisely as you see it here. CSS needs to use this specific format, or it won't work. The background in Twine stories is black by default, but you could change it to any color you want: `blue`, `green`, `purple`, `hotpink`, or `indigo`. (You'll find a more extensive list of HTML color names at *http://html-color-names.com/color-chart.php/*). Test-play your story to see the new background color.

Stylizing Your Text

Next, I changed the passage color in the *Ghost Burgers* stylesheet to white using this code:

```
tw-passage
{
  color: white;
}
```

The code `tw-passage` is short for "Twine passage," and it contains information about how your story's passages will look.

You can change more than just the color. For example, you can change the font family and size by adding something like this:

```
tw-passage
{
  font-family: Courier New;
  font-size: 40px;
  color: hotpink;
}
```

This code changes the font to Courier New, the font size to 40, and the color of all the text in all the passages to hot pink, which looks like this.

"You only have 3 pebbles! The toll is *five*!" says the royal guard. Maybe there are some pebbles you missed at the **old creek**.

Adding Fancy Touches

You can also change the width of your text display, which is like an invisible box that contains your story's words, and add a fancy border. Try adding the following to `tw-passage`:

```
  width: 500px;
  border: dashed blue;
```

Your display should show a dashed blue border 500 pixels wide.

```
You're at the top of
a hill. I guess you
might call it a
hilltop. From this
high up you can see
everything around
you for miles, but
there isn't much to
see, really, other
than the old creek
and the fairy
kingdom.
```

> **NOTE:** *Pixels* are the tiny dots that make up the image on your computer screen. The word *pixel* comes from picture elements, and it's abbreviated as px (for example, 500px means 500 pixels).

You can change the color of the links in your game, too. For example, if you wanted to make your links crimson, you would enter this code

```
tw-link
{
  color: crimson;
}
```

To learn more about what you can change on the stylesheet, see the Twine **Help** page. (Click **Help** on the Twine Stories page, and then click **Change the Font, Colors, or Appearance**.)

Opening Ghost Burgers' Source Files

If you're not sure how I created some of the features in this game, you can look at the game's *source code*. To do that, open *Ghost Burgers* in your web browser by navigating to *https://nostarch.com/twinegames/*, right-click on the background of the web page (or Control-click if you're using a Mac), and click **Save as**. Make sure you right-click the actual page and then save it to your computer. Then, on your Twine Stories page at *http://twinery.org/2/#!/stories/*, click **Import From File** to open the *Ghost Burgers.html* file you saved in Twine.

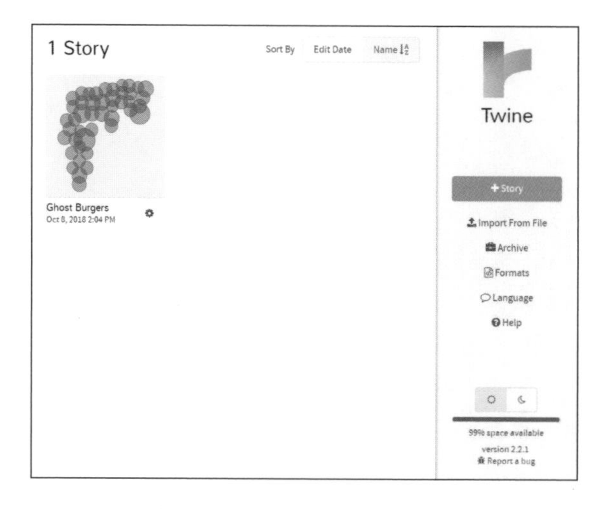

Now you can look at the guts of *Ghost Burgers*, as shown here.

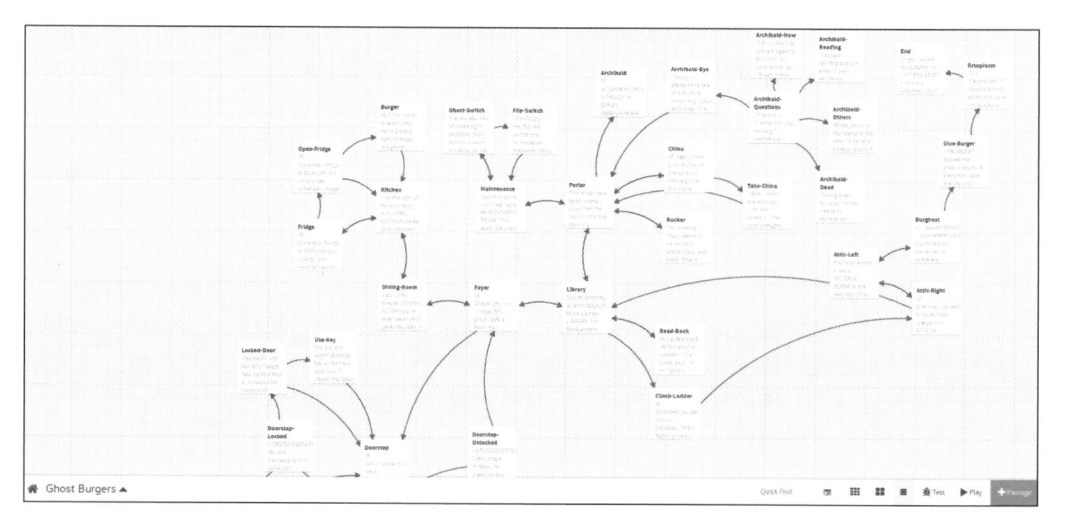

Double-click the passages to see how I made them work and which hooks I used. You can do this for any of the example games in this book. In fact, you can do this for most Twine games. Just remember that although it's perfectly okay to look inside someone's Twine game to see how they made something, it's not okay to copy someone's work without asking them! Be respectful when you're having a look-see at other peoples' creations!

As you dig through the *Ghost Burgers* code, you'll find a few techniques I haven't explained, like how I made the cobwebs in the attic. I made those using the `Click-replace` hook and named hooks. A *named hook* is just a name that you give to a specific hook so *another* hook can do something to it. For example, clicking a link at the bottom of the page can change a piece of text near the top of the page. Look inside the *Attic* passage and see if you can figure out how they work. (You'll find information on named hooks and all other hooks in Twine at *http://twine2.neocities.org/)*.

Don't be afraid to try hooks in your own stories!

What You Learned

Now you know how to make more sophisticated Twine games. You can keep track of what the player has read so that you can change what the player sees, and you know how to change your story's appearance. You're a programmer now—congratulations! From now on, your Twine games can be as simple or complicated as you want them to be.

In Chapter 4, we'll work with more advanced techniques. If the information is more complicated than you're comfortable with, feel free to skip to the game challenges in Chapter 5! Programming is not for everyone, and that's fine!

4

Pebble Economy: Using Variables to Count Items

In the previous chapter, you used some basic Twine techniques to add text effects, display a random selection from a list of book titles, and link to a menu of passage links. You learned about Boolean variables that have two different values, which you used with conditionals to make decisions in your game. You also learned how to use integer variables to assign different events to specific conditions. In this chapter, you'll build on what you learned to create more complicated scripts and discover what variables are really capable of!

This chapter is a short one. If it seems like a little too much to wrap your head around, don't be afraid to skip it. Maybe you'll come back to it when you have more experience scripting in Twine and want to try some more advanced stuff!

Counting Fairy Pebbles

Similar to regular numbers, you can use *integer* variables to add, subtract, and check how low or high their value is. You might also use an integer variable to count the number of cats the player has petted or to remember how many sandwiches the player has made for their picnic. Let's explore how to keep track of the number of pebbles the player is carrying around using a game called *The Pebble Economy*.

The Pebble Economy contains an example of how you might use integer variable numbers in Twine. In this short game, the player has to find enough pebbles to pay a fairy toll: it costs five pebbles to enter the Fairy Kingdom. Check out the game at *https://nostarch.com/twinegames/*.

You feel along the bottom of the creek with your hand and manage to scoop up two pebbles! One of them is shiny and the other one is lumpy.

You have 6 pebbles.

Do you want to try and **look for more pebbles**? Or you could head over to the **fairy kingdom**?

We'll use the variable `$pebbles` to track the number of pebbles the player has found.

Each time the player searches for pebbles at the old creek, they find one, two, three, or zero pebbles (they find a weird frog instead), which are added to their total. We use `display` and `either` to randomly choose the passage the player sees, which determines the number of pebbles they find. As you learned in Chapter 3, you can use `either` to choose a random passage and `display` to make the contents of that passage appear. Each passage gives the player a different number of pebbles.

For example, we can use the following line to add two new pebbles the player has found in a passage to their total number of pebbles:

```
(set: $pebbles to $pebbles + 2)
```

This line tells Twine to set `$pebbles` to the current value of `$pebbles` plus 2. So if the value of `$pebbles` was 2, this line's value would increase to 4.

To display the value of a variable, just enter its name in a sentence to show the player how many pebbles they have:

```
You have $pebbles pebbles.
```

This line displays the total number using the value stored in the `$pebbles` variable. The player should see "You have 4 pebbles," "You have 10 pebbles," or "You have 500 pebbles," depending on how many pebbles the player has found up to that point.

Using elseif to Check Integer Values

It makes sense to use `if` and `else` for Booleans because they're either true or false, on or off. If they're not one value, they must be the other. But integers can have more than two possibilities. For example, you might have enough pebbles to pay the toll. You might have no pebbles at all! Or you might have *some* pebbles but not enough! That's three different conditions to check for, which means that using `if` and `else` alone isn't going to cut it!

Fortunately, we can use `elseif` to keep track of a third value:

```
{
(if: $pebbles >= 5)[You have enough pebbles!]
(elseif: $pebbles is 0)[You don't have ANY pebbles!]
(else:)[You only have $pebbles pebbles!]
}
```

The `elseif` statement works like a regular `if` statement with an additional condition! In this example, Twine first checks whether `$pebbles` is greater than or equal to 5 using the hook `(if: $pebbles >= 5)`.

If `$pebbles` is greater than or equal to 5, Twine displays "You have enough pebbles!" and that's that. But if it isn't, Twine tries the `elseif` hook `(elseif: $pebbles is 0)` to check if `$pebbles` is equal to 0. If it is, Twine displays "You don't have ANY pebbles!" to let the player know they need more pebbles.

If neither condition is true, then Twine moves on to the `else` statement. The `else` part covers every possible case other than those covered by the `if` and `elseif`, which is when the player has 1, 2, 3, and 4 pebbles. We tell Twine to display `[You only have $pebbles pebbles!]`, where `$pebbles` represents the number of pebbles the player has.

The Order of Things Is Important!

Keep in mind that the order in which you write your code is important. When Twine decides what code to execute, and in what order to do it, it reads from top to bottom, the same way you read a page in this book.

When you write code for your games, make sure it's written in the order that will make the most sense in Twine. For example, we write the `else` statement at the very end because we want Twine to do this only after checking the first two conditions.

But what if you want an additional condition? You might want to add an encouraging message if the player is *really* close to having enough pebbles for the toll. We can update the existing code with another `elseif` statement like this:

```
{
(if: $pebbles >= 5)[You have enough pebbles!]
(elseif: $pebbles >= 3)[You have $pebbles pebbles! Almost
there!]
(elseif: $pebbles is 0)[You don't have ANY pebbles!]
(else:)[You only have $pebbles pebbles!]
}
```

Now there's a different message for the player when they have 3 or more pebbles. Notice that we put the `elseif` statement second from the top. That's because if we put this `elseif` statement before the `if` statement, a player would see the "Almost there!" message even when they had 6 pebbles because 6 is *also* greater than or equal to 3. But that doesn't make sense, because the player already has enough pebbles to pay the toll! Only if the player *doesn't* have at least 5 pebbles do we want Twine to check whether they have 3 or more.

Twine always starts by checking the `if` case. Then it checks each of the `elseif` statements in order from top to bottom. You can write as many `elseif` statements as you want. As soon as Twine finds a condition that is true, Twine stops there and does what you told it to do in that case. If none of the `elseif` statements are true, *only then* does it check for the `else`. The `else` statement is Twine's last resort.

Whenever code you've written doesn't work the way you expected, read through your code from top to bottom to check that your conditions are in the right order. Perhaps Twine stopped before it got to the case you expected because an earlier condition was also true. Sometimes, simply rearranging the order in which Twine looks for conditions can solve a problem.

String Variables

Strings are a type of variable that contains text: a word, phrase, or sentence. Your Twine games are mostly text already, but sometimes you'll need to keep track of a *particular* piece of text. For example, you can use string variables to keep track of whether the player put on a "red baseball cap" or a "plastic tiara" before leaving the house this morning.

To see a string variable in action, enter the following:

```
{
(set: $hat to "plastic baseball tiara")
The wind is so strong that your $hat is blown right off your
head!
}
```

Try hitting play! Twine should print "The wind is so strong that your plastic baseball tiara is blown right off your head!" Try changing the description of the hat. The game should change to match what you typed!

The important thing is that you make sure there are quotes (") on either side of the string. That's how Twine knows where the string starts and stops. If it's inside the quotes, it's a string. If it's outside, it's code.

Can you think of how this technique might be useful in a story? Maybe the game starts in the player's bedroom, where a few of their favorite hats are hanging. Whatever hat they choose, you can set $hat to match the description of the hat. That way when the story mentions the player's hat, it can mention the specific one that they chose!

You could ask them to pick their favorite color. You could ask whether they'd like a pet cat or a pet dog. There's a piece of code that will let the player type something in—you can ask them to name their pet, then refer to the pet by the name they chose! Read through the Twine wiki and see if you can figure out how.

A Note on Story Formats

In this book, I use Twine 2's default story format, which is Harlowe. Twine 2 has two other story formats: Snowman and SugarCube. To change your game's story format, click its name, and then choose Change Story Format. But keep in mind that all the hooks you've learned so far are specific to Harlowe. Other story formats can do the same things, but the code you'll need to write will be a little different.

You'll find plenty of information about story formats at *http://twine2.neocities.org/* and on Twine's Help page.

What You Learned

In this rather short chapter, you learned more about how variables work and how you can change what's stored inside them. In particular, you learned that integer variables contain numbers and that string variables contain words or phrases.

In the next and final chapter, I'll show you more Twine games that you can play (created by people other than me!) as well as provide you with some challenges to try in your own game design practice.

5

Where to Go from Here

You made it to the final chapter! How does it feel to be a game designer? A little weird? Don't worry—that's normal. Maybe you don't *feel* like a game designer yet. That's normal too.

It's easy to feel like you're not qualified to call yourself something. But there are so many different ways to be a game designer. For example, game designers can be people who work at big companies where everyone makes small contributions to a product. Game designers can also be people who sit in their bedrooms making things that they find fun.

Game designers are also people who go to the park to play catch with friends, and then wonder, "What if we have to toss the ball under our leg?" or "What if we're not allowed to touch the ball with our hands?" There are a million-and-a-half different ways to be a game designer.

Asking Questions

You might not have a ton of game design experience yet, but I'll tell you a cool fact about game design: if you're doing it right, it should *always* remain a mystery to you. Even the people who've designed games for years are still asking questions about what games could be. "What if you can only move one space every day?" "What kind of game can you play at a protest?" "Why don't games let you make friends with the monsters instead of fighting them?"

Game design is less about finding answers than it is about asking questions. Everyone, regardless of their skill level and experience, can ask questions.

In this chapter, I'll show you some cool Twine games other people have made as well as provide you with some exercises to try when you're making your own games.

More Twine Games to Try

You learned how to build some Twine games from scratch and share them online. Even if you don't think your game is perfect, you should be proud that you've *made something*. Many adults who have been making games for way longer than you still have a hard time finishing them.

But this is only your first Twine game. What will your next one be like? Keep your mind open so new ideas can get in. Ideas might find you when you're walking in the park, when you're staring at the ceiling over your bed, or even when you're in the bathroom. Never be too quick to dismiss a daydream; it could be the seed for an amazing game!

In the meantime, here are a few more Twine game examples you can try to see what's possible with Twine; perhaps you'll want to make a similar Twine game.

Candy Ant Princess by Whisperbat

In *Candy Ant Princess*, you get to make lots of little decisions that don't change the game much but help you feel like the story you're playing is your own story. Try it now at *https://tinyurl.com/candyant*.

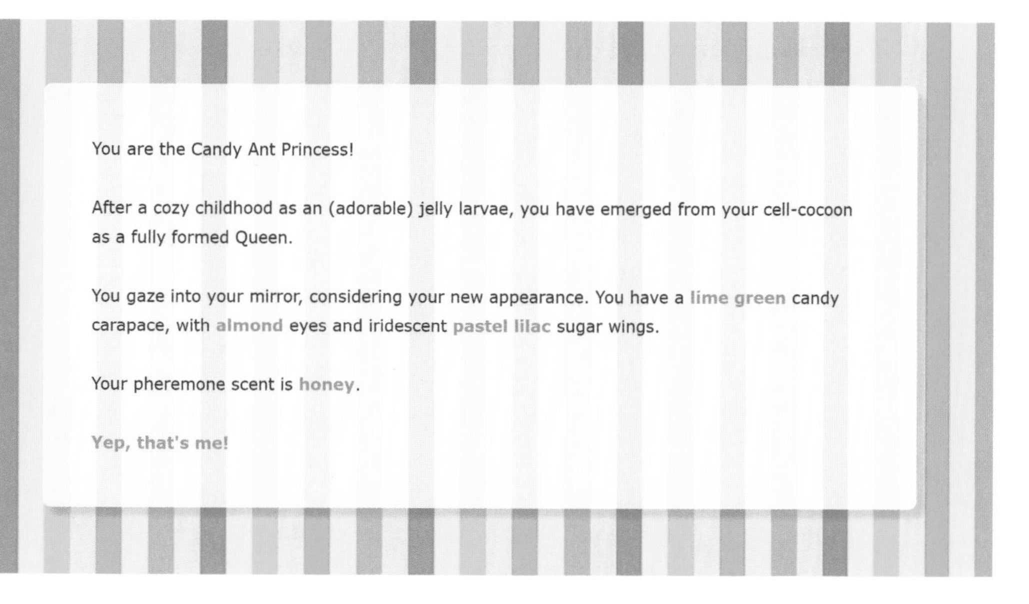

You can choose what your candy ant princess looks like, what kind of candy pet you have, and where you make your candy ant nest. These small details help you decide what your candy ant princess is like and how she sees herself in candy ant society.

The Message by Jeremy Lonien and Dominik Johann

The Message is a short game that manages to build up a lot of suspense before—well, I don't want to spoil the ending! This game uses text formatting and pictures in very smart ways to help create its mood. Cleverly, it also provides a link to a YouTube video full of space sounds recorded by NASA that you can leave open as a soundtrack while you play the game. Check it out at *http://ludonaut.de/the-message/*.

A Bucket Filled with Sand by A. C. Godliman

A Bucket Filled with Sand is a game about history, destiny, and sandcastles (*http://tinyurl.com/bucketsand/*). It uses lots of pictures to show how your sand kingdom grows and changes. It's a good example of a game in which little choices you make between one option and another lead you down different branches and paths. You might need to give the game a minute to load all the pictures.

Sometimes when you look at stuff other people have made, you can easily get discouraged. You might think to yourself, "Well, that's way better than anything I could make." I know, because I think that all the time.

But there's another way to think about the cool things other people make. You could say, "Wow, I didn't know you could do that! But now I do! The next thing I make will be *so much cooler* because of it!"

The more you explore other people's games, the more likely you'll be to think of ideas and designs you've never thought of before, and the more you'll learn about what you can make. In fact, every little thing you learn about or play with can make you better at creating your own games because they help fuel new ideas during the planning stage.

So don't let other peoples' art scare you into thinking you can't do something similarly cool. Give yourself permission to learn from others' work. The more Twine games you play, the more ideas you'll get! I've been making games with Twine for years, and I'm still coming up with more ideas.

Game Challenges

When you're done exploring these games, here are some exercises you can try. Some of them are about challenging yourself to make a game in a new way. Some challenge you to promote your games and work with others. Each challenge starts with a question. And each of those questions, hopefully, will lead you to ask more questions of your own.

Don't worry about completing every one or doing them in order. Do the ones that most excite you and lead you to the most interesting questions.

Write a Story to Fit a Cool Shape

In previous chapters, you learned how to write a Twine story and then rearrange the passages into a cool shape, like a lightning bolt or spiral.

For this challenge, try reversing the process. For example, come up with the overall shape of your Twine blueprint first by creating passages before writing in them. Then go back and fill in the passages to create a story. Let the shape of the story guide what you write! What would be in a Twine game shaped like a heart? Or a star? How would the passages connect?

This approach might seem counterintuitive, but it'll challenge you to write more creatively. If you're stuck in a rut and are having trouble coming up with a new idea, a challenge like this could be just what you need to shake some ideas loose.

Tell a Story with Just Pictures

For this challenge, you'll need a way to get your drawings onto a computer if you prefer to draw by hand. Or you can just draw them right on your computer using a paint program.

Now, can you write a Twine story that's all pictures with no text whatsoever? (It's okay if the links are words.) If you're not sure where to begin, here's a fun idea: using a game you've already written in words, translate it into pictures. How is the game design process different or similar? For example, how do you provide different choices to the player using a picture?

TIP: Instead of uploading your images one by one to *https://postimage.org/*, which is tedious, why not register a *https://neocities.org/* page for your game and upload all the images there at once?

Make Your Twine Story into a Booklet!

Try making a paper version of your Twine game to share with your friends. For example, in a physical version of your game, instead of using links, you might need to tell the reader to turn to page 4 or page 15. How would your story be different when someone is holding it in their hands instead of playing it on a computer? What can you do on paper that's hard to do on the computer?

One cool idea would be to tell a riddle and have the reader turn the page upside down to read the answer. If you draw a comic book and number all the panels, you can tell the reader to go to a specific panel. You can even leave a blank spot for them to write in their own ending!

Collaborate with Friends

Try making a game with a friend. It can be very exciting to bounce ideas back and forth with someone else. Each of you can build on what the other has come up with. Some of the most powerful ideas emerge that way, and the energy of collaboration can be really fun.

There are a lot of different ways to work together on a project. For example, you can write the first half of the game, and your friend can write the second part. Or maybe you write the passage descriptions, and your partner writes the links. You could write the story, and someone else could draw the pictures. Maybe you could just have someone read your story and offer ideas.

Working with other people on creative projects can be tricky, especially when they're your friends. If you get into an argument about the project, it could affect your friendship outside of it. Collaborating feels great when you both have the same level of energy and excitement, but tensions can build when you both have different amounts of energy or availability. At times, you might see one person taking charge of the whole project and making all the decisions.

Collaboration is all about communication! If someone doesn't feel like they're involved enough in decision making or feels frustrated because they think they're spending more time on the project than the other person, have a conversation about it! Offer constructive criticism without getting defensive: try to be specific about what the problem is, how it makes you feel, and what could make the situation better.

Collaboration is a lot of work, but it can lead to amazing things you couldn't make on your own.

Make a Journal Game

Have you ever kept a journal? *Journaling* is when you write down what happened that day, what was important about it, how it made you feel, and why. What if you tried to make a game from your journal? For example, how would you make something that happened to you interactive?

You can make a journal game about almost anything! Moving to a new town. Having a little sister. Making friends with a cat. Being different. Winning a spelling bee. Losing a spelling bee. Breaking your arm. Or just watching the sunset. Games don't always have to be about spider milk and ghost burgers. They can be about you, too!

Because a journal game can be very personal, think about what you're comfortable sharing with other people and what you want to keep to yourself. You can certainly make a game that's meant just for you: what would that look like? What about a game you make to share with just one friend? Not every game is for everyone.

Make Games with Bitsy

Bitsy is a cute little game maker by Adam Le Doux. Like Twine, Bitsy lets you write words and put them in a game. It also lets you draw little characters, scenery, and animation and make little worlds out of them. If you want to take what you've done with Twine and add a more *visual* dimension to it, Bitsy could be a fun next step!

You can find the Bitsy editor online at *http://tinyurl.com/bitsyeditor/*. For an example of what you can do with Bitsy, try playing the game *You Have to Go to Work* by KC at *http://tinyurl.com/bitsywork/*.

Keep Exploring and Creating!

The world we live in is not always the best place, and it can be easy to lose hope and joy. Making art—whether that's games, comics, zines, music, stories, or just a little garden in your window—helps us remember that we're capable of creating beautiful things. It reminds us to feel wonder for our surroundings and ourselves.

The older you get, the less time you have for play and creating things that don't make money. Get in the habit of making and doing, and hold onto it as you grow older! It's never too late to start. Making art will increase your enjoyment for life. *For real.*

But this book is just a starting point. Now that you know how to make games using Twine, it's up to you to figure out what to do with that knowledge. Follow your ideas wherever they lead you, even if they seem silly, weird, or unoriginal. Keep exploring.

I can't wait to see what you come up with.

Index

Symbols

A

B

C

D

E